CHARACTER MATTERS

~

NINE ESSENTIAL TRAITS YOU NEED *to* SUCCEED

~

MARK RUTLAND

100 Huntley Street

crossroads
FAMILY OF MINISTRIES

CHARACTER MATTERS by Mark Rutland
Published by Charisma House
A Strang Company
600 Rinehart Road
Lake Mary, Florida 32746
www.charismahouse.com

Unless otherwise noted, all Scripture quotations are from the King James Version of the Bible.

Scripture quotations marked ASV are from the American Standard Version of the Bible. Public domain.

Scripture quotations marked NIV are from the Holy Bible, New International Version. Copyright © 1973, 1978, 1984, International Bible Society. Used by permission.

Cover design by The Office of Bill Chiaravalle | www.officeofbc.com
Cover photo by Photodisc
Interior design by David Bilby

International Standard Book Number: 1-59185-915-8

Special Crossroads Partner Edition

05 06 07 08 09 — 8 7 6 5 4 3 2 1
Printed in the United States of America

Dedicated

to

the students and alumni

of

Southeastern College

Lakeland, Florida

ACKNOWLEDGMENTS

Behind every successful man there is a surprised mother-in-law. Likewise, behind every published book there are a multiplicity of eyes and hands and minds, other than the author's, whose contributions were indispensable. Though my name alone appears on the jacket, and, indeed, I wrote every word of it, I feel it is only fitting that they who assisted should have to share the blame.

My wife, my Alison, who patiently lets me read to her what I write, whose editorial suggestions are invaluable, must be thanked first. I am as sane as I am, or perhaps I should say, I am no more insane than I am, because her beauty, balance and brains keep me from drifting out to sea. My high school sweetheart, the smartest woman I know, and the love of my life, she is in and behind every word.

Because I remain, in this cyber age, a belligerent Neanderthal, unable to type, let alone use a computer, my undying gratitude belongs to Dr. Gordon Miller and Mrs. Glenna Rakes for their help in editing and preparing the manuscript. I take a salacious delight in watching an empty page fill up with my handwritten words, but their ability to decipher the meaning of that scrawl is nothing short of miraculous.

Barbara Dycus and all her colleagues at Charisma House do not escape responsibility. They also contributed greatly to this effort and did so deliberately with grace and good humor. So that Barbara cannot later deny involvement, her name is also recorded here with my thanks.

CONTENTS

v

CHAPTER 1

CHARACTER:
THE ENGRAVER'S ART

———————— ∾ ————————

A man's character is his fate.

—HERACLITUS

———————— ∾ ————————

THE ENGLISH WORD *CHARACTER* IS from a Latin root that means "engraved." A life, like a block of granite carved upon with care or hacked at with reckless disregard, will, at the end, be either a masterpiece or marred rubble. Character, the composite of virtues and values etched in that living stone, will define its true worth. No cosmetic enhancement, no decorative drapery can make useless stone into enduring art. Only character can do that.

A nation having squandered its character may well have so damaged itself that attempts at reclamation prove futile. Long before that final collapse, however, redoubts can be built and buttressed against the invading armies of the night. Virtues can be revisited, rethought and retaught. From a nation's pulpits and podia, in its businesses and on its forts, a corporate voice calling for character may turn the tide.

Children can be taught courage. Executives, suckled on the milk of Gordon Gecko's greed, can be reminded of honesty and frugality. Modesty can be learned, valued and lived where a nation will find its voice and teach it once again. For now we are reaping the bitter harvest of character

1

destruction, but it is not too late.

Character embraced, even popularized and freshly articu-
lated in our literature and movies, will produce leaders upon
whose lives words like *honesty*, *gratitude* and *courage* have
been engraved with faith and hope. It is not too late for character. We have the right as a free people to expect it, even
demand it, in our leaders. We have the responsibility to cultivate it in ourselves, to teach it in our schools and to praise
and reward it in others.

What we engrave or allow to be engraved upon us is what
we must live with. Talent, attractiveness and intellect, too
long overvalued, have proven incapable of re-firing our
national hope. The Bill Clintons of this society have chipped
away valuable and irreplaceable granite. Now we need more
modest athletes, meeker leaders, honest executives and more
diligent workers.

A new national character, new only in the narrowest of
historical views, can be, and must be, engraved. The granite
of us, worn and pocked as it is, can still receive the well-
guided stylus. Character matters, and now is the time.

Why Enron? Why the whole Clinton-Lewinsky quagmire?
Why any of it?

The problem is, those are actually the wrong questions,
both wrong and easy to answer. Scandal, crime and wicked-
ness in high and low places are in the fallenness of us. Sin is.
That is the simple and terrifying answer to both the murderous mayhem in our streets and the shocking deceptions in
our board rooms.

The real question is, How can character be added back
into an American soul adrift on a Sargasso Sea of postmodern relativism? It is not that there have never before
been scandals. From the Hamilton-Burr duel to the Teapot
Dome to Watergate, the highway of American history is littered with trash. In the past, however, scandal was, at least,
well, scandalous. Now little, if anything, is fixed, absolutely

wrong or absolutely right. Our ability, as a people, to be scandalized by anything is being frittered away.

Not the movies, not the art or the music or the literature, but the character of a culture is its defining nexus, that which holds it together, the place where all its dots connect and make it what it is. When the character of any culture loses its grip on the essential virtues that hold the whole thing in place, the scandals still happen, but the culture is no longer outraged.

Indeed, in the Clinton-Lewinsky debacle, the background music of the president's defense was that his ability as a president combined with a good economy made perjury and adultery non-issues. Likewise, when the Enron disaster burst open, we could hardly bring ourselves to even speak of the greed and dissembling. The greater issue was perceived to be the financial loss to employees and investors.

In other words, the inescapable conclusion is that when there is no substantial financial loss, it is not a real scandal. This was even stated by one speaker who said, "The real sin is not the president's sexual habits, but the money Ken Starr spent on the prosecution."

Character, the inner moral strength of a people, is a factor of all that is loved, admired, despised and taught to its young. A culture rests on its virtues, and virtues can be taught. It is not too late for us to teach character again. Indeed, amidst the cacophonous jabberwocky that would mock the greatest virtues of our historical culture, I hear a rising voice that says, "Character matters."

A number of years ago Dr. Karl Menninger wrote *Whatever Became of Sin?* The book was a call to personal accountability. To be sure, Menninger did not believe that sin itself had disappeared. He referred to the virtual disappearance of the concept and the word from our vocabulary. He meant, "Whatever became of the idea of sin?"—not that we are short of it.[1]

With this book I am asking another question: Whatever became of character? The whole concept of virtuous living has become so alien to Western culture that until—and unless—we recapture it, our society will remain unengraved with character.

Far too long now our society has tended to think of virtue as a quality desirable only for women. We are led to think that women should be virginal and good, at least the ones men marry, but men are to be somehow above such sissy notions. Such thinking may be convenient for men, but it reveals a tragic misunderstanding of true virtue.

The very word *virtue* derives from the Latin word for strength. The connotation is of straining, as the muscles of a man might strain at the confines of a tight shirt. In other words, virtue is restrained strength. It actually implies manliness. It is that strength, that power by which one physical body affects another. In medicine there is a classical use of the word *virtue*. The virtue of a plant, for example, is that power inherent in it to produce medicine. Virtue also relates to the medicine itself. There is virtue in the medicine for healing. Mixture, adulteration, dilution or exposure may diminish the virtue.

In the eighth chapter of his Gospel, Luke used the word *virtue* to connote power. A woman with an abnormal flow of blood came near to Jesus, struggling in the crowd just to touch His garment. Jesus announced to those around Him that someone had touched Him. In the wild, unruly jostling, such a statement seemed absurd. How could He tell one touch from another? Jesus explained that He felt *virtue* flow out of Him.

There is power in virtue and virtue in power. Resident in the virtuous is inestimable power to impact others for good. Character matters, and virtue is the strength of character.

THE DOWNWARD SPIRAL

Every society anchors its ideals in its virtues. If those virtues are good, it is ennobled. When those virtues are absent or perverted, there will be a downward spiral in the values, actions and character of its people.

The real danger is not the absence of virtue. There is no historical evidence of an utterly virtueless society. The great danger is not the lack of any virtue. It is wrong virtues! It is always tragic when men who understand virtue act in virtue-less ways, but the greater danger is redefining virtue as evil and evil as virtue. When that happens, the power that holds civilization intact is weakened.

In ancient Rome a preeminent virtue was bravery. Roman bravery, misunderstood and untempered by Christian love, soon became brutal and callous. Similarly, in communist Russia, for many years, the zenith of all virtue was loyalty to the state. That virtue was perverted into a lethal poison that pumped shattered lives into Siberia like the pathetic waste of socialistic atheism. The Stalinist state expected its citizens to betray family members even if it meant death or imprisonment. Stalin professed that any lie, any act of treachery, any form of violence was acceptable—even virtuous—in the cause of communism. Torture, deceit and murder were not seen as violations of virtue. Instead they actually became the vehicles by which Stalin's preeminent virtue was celebrated.

As a society defines its virtues, it in turn is defined by those virtues. Twisted virtue means twisted culture. Suppose, for example, a certain society hates failure, ugliness, obesity and stupidity. The premier virtues might then be success, beauty and intelligence. If, therefore, beauty itself is a virtue, then all is permissible if I can achieve beauty, associate with beauty or cause beauty to be.

The downward spiral might go something like this:

1. Beauty as an abstract ascends as a societal virtue.

2. If beauty is a virtue, ugliness is despicable.

3. If ugliness is despicable, ugly people are worth less than beautiful people.

4. If beautiful people are worth more than ugly people, it is not as bad to murder the ugly.

5. Finally, murdering ugly people may, at last, be seen as virtuous.

By just such a perverted spiral, a society might embrace even murder in the pursuit of beauty. Some may object that such a scenario is bizarre and farfetched. It is, in fact, quite reasonable.

The society in which beauty is the highest virtue could easily degenerate to the point where pornography would be held in higher regard than the Bible. Imagine a society so degraded that art of any kind would be held in higher regard than chastity or mercy. That society might well permit or even commission its artists to produce the most heinous kinds of evil in the name of art. A state that will subsidize urine portraits of Jesus might allow portraits of Mary painted in the blood of virgins. At the end of the day, murder for art's sake may not be as farfetched as we think.

VIRTUE AND VITALITY

If a society hopes to elevate or ennoble its character, it must carefully define its virtues. The most basic values held by a society dictate the kind of leaders it will produce. If the premier values are hard work, perseverance, ingenuity and discipline, that society produces men like George Washington Carver. On the other hand, if the preeminent virtue is wealth—no matter how you get it—Enron is the inevitable result.

A survey of mothers of school-age children was conducted

in both Japan and the United States. It asked this question: What do you consider the most important variable in a child's success in school? By far the largest number of American mothers thought it to be intelligence. Almost 100 percent of the Japanese mothers, however, answered far more wisely that work and diligence will make the difference.

I well remember the shocking experience of explaining the heroic ethos to a group of American school children. Using the plot of the old Western movie *High Noon*, I told them the story of the hero who single-handedly, for the sake of a cowardly, undeserving town, faced an entire gang of outlaws. His bride, a nice enough girl, did not admire or stand by him and declared that she believed him to be a fool. Then I told them of the moment of truth when, all alone, our hero had to settle things in the street.

"What do you think of a guy like that?" I asked.

One ten-year-old boy answered at once, "Whatta sucker!"

I cringed. That child had already begun to redefine the virtue of courage so that, in his mind, it no longer included selfless love. I doubted if I could explain the courage of the cross to that boy.

The teenager who makes rebellion a virtue imitates rebellious men. The way he stands and dresses, what he does and refuses to do, the things he will and will not endure betray his real virtues. The businessman who sells tainted baby food to a Third World country without a qualm knows that his society has defined a virtue called *success without integrity*. A congressman who makes power a virtue sells his soul for votes, awaiting the crest of every political poll like an ideological surfer. It is, above all things, courage that separates men from the beasts.

Likewise, the prevailing winds of virtue greatly impact whether the church in a society produces an Elmer Gantry or a John Wesley. If that which we as a people admire is flamboyant success in a worldly sense, the local pastor must

live on the highest level of personal commitment to virtue,
or he will succumb to this lowest level of ambition. He must
fight the weight of materialism, struggle to resist compromise and defeat fear.

During the war in Iraq I saw a protestor with a sign reading,
"THERE IS NOTHING WORTH DYING FOR." Now,
there may well be nothing worth killing for. That is a different
thing. "There is nothing worth dying for" is the motto of the
beastly instinct to survive at any cost! There must be people or
ideas worth dying for. If not, the cross is a sick joke, and
Tiananmen Square was a parade of fools.

The character of any society will be dictated by how it
defines its virtues. A woman in New England shot to death
her four-year-old son. Though she was found guilty, her
judge probated the five-year sentence. The judge said that
while it was indeed murder, it was mitigated by the fact that
the boy was retarded. Now is the winter of our discontent!
America is staring into the abyss when legal decisions concerning the fundamental sanctity of life are handed down by
those whose sense of virtue is based upon expediency and
convenience.

Some years ago I engaged in a radio debate about abortion. My opponent was a pro-choice rabbi. He explained that
he rejected the old idea of the value of life. He calmly
announced that he now held "quality of life" to be a higher
ideal. I was stunned! I could hardly look at him. It was hard
to believe what I was hearing. I asked if he realized that he
had just uttered the same words used by the Nazi judges to
justify the forced sterilization of the retarded and the killing
of the Jews and Gypsies. He was furious, of course, and the
debate lost all hope of any usefulness.

Afterward, in the parking lot, the rabbi screamed at me,
"Are you daring to call *me* a Nazi?" I assured him I was not,
but I went on to say that the world is topside-down when
rabbis think like Nazis.

Something was terribly wrong with his reasoning. Our ideal cannot be the quality of life. That puts comfort, ease, beauty, intelligence, wealth, power and convenience ahead of decency, goodness, kindness and the innate value of every life created by God. The *quality* of life cannot be more important than the *value* of life. If the quality of life is the prime consideration, who defines quality? Perhaps all the mothers of the mentally deficient will be allowed to obtain a license to do away with any children who cause the family a lower quality of life. If we can hire doctors to abort unborn babies, then the next step may be clinics where we can quite legally murder the elderly or inconvenient. When society accepts convenience and the quality of life as more precious than life itself, the only really valuable people are those who pander to culture's lusts or provide its needs.

VIRTUE: FAITH AND WORKS

In an adolescent overreaction to "works" righteousness, many modern Christians have an unreasonable disdain of any human effort to reach for maturity and wholeness. To be sure, we cannot bring ourselves into right standing with God. Only the blood of Jesus can do that. As Paul writes, "By grace you have been saved, through faith—and this not from yourselves, it is the gift of God—not by works, so that no one can boast" (Eph. 2:8–9, NIV).

Yet it was the apostle Peter who said, "Add to your faith virtue" (2 Pet. 1:5).

There is a covenant between the man of God and the God of man that implies life at both ends. Let me give you a parable. Here is a tree, a stone and the sun. The sun rises and says, "Let us make a covenant; I will shine on you, and you respond to me." Can the sun make such a covenant with a stone? Certainly not! The stone has no life; it cannot grow. The stone cannot mature or develop. What about the tree? Certainly the greater power is with the sun. It is the energy and the influence. The tree, however, can respond to all the sun has to offer. Its response is summoned by the sun, but, unlike the stone, it will twist and reach to grow in the rays of power.

The same thing is true of the Christian. The psalmist wrote, "Trust in him and he will do this: he will make your righteousness shine like the dawn" (Ps. 37:5–6, NIV). We dare not sit like the stone, hardened against the Son of righteousness. In other words, God's willingness to help us must be met with our willingness to be helped. We must add virtue to faith. We must purpose in our hearts for God to teach us true virtue so that it permeates the inner man and becomes the illuminating influence of our lives. In an age of virtueless wolves ranging the land in packs, the man of God must seek illumination. God can teach us virtue, but we must want it. Perhaps a hundred years ago in the West, a book on character might have been so obvious as to have seemed frivolous. There would hardly have been a need to teach or write on virtue. God said the Ninevites did not know their right hand from their left. Perhaps the same might be said of modern America. America has lost her basic concept of virtue.

It is time to demand virtue of ourselves, our courts, our government and our entire society. With our virtue squandered, we are doomed to life on the jungle floor. We must struggle for virtue now, in our generation.

It is time, but it is not too late. Character can still be taught, modeled and cultivated. The threads of virtue can still be found and used to weave a tapestry of character, but we must be intentional and creative. New ways of understanding and teaching character must be explored and used in schools, businesses and places of worship.

Now is the time for character. Persons of virtue with the power to touch this tired culture with transforming grace will not just happen. We must be intentional to produce them, teach them and carve them with care on the soul of a nation. We can and have lived with less wealth than we have. We have survived stock market crashes, depressions and world wars. We cannot long survive without character. Now, not later—for there may, in fact, be no later—now is the time for character.

CHAPTER 2

COURAGE:
CHARACTER IN CRISIS

The Bradley armored vehicle inched its way onto the bridge. Three soldiers, Americans, young with everything to live for, crouched low as they followed, their eyes on the old woman. Bullets from the Iraqi guns on the far side of the river pinged off the sides of the vehicle and the steel girders of the bridge. The soldiers kept coming, risking their lives with every step, braving the enemy guns, all for the life of the elderly Iraqi woman huddled in the gun smoke.

The officer in charge tossed a smoke grenade, and three Americans ran forward to pull the woman to safety. Captain Chris Carter, at the ripe old age of thirty-one, was the company commander. He ordered his men to retreat, carrying the woman, while he gave covering fire with an M-16.

On March 31, 2003, Captain Chris Carter and his men acted courageously on a bridge somewhere south of Baghdad. They were not merely brave, but courageous, risking their lives for a defenseless woman in danger from the bullets of her nation's army.[1]

~

Courage is the ladder on which all the other virtues mount.

—Clara Booth Luce

~

THE MISGUIDED, THE DECEIVED AND the fanatical may at times act bravely, hurling themselves into the jaws of death. True courage—noble courage, the authentic spontaneous act of self-sacrificial concern for the defenseless—is not fanaticism but character.

The way a society comprehends courage will, in a great part, determine whether it will be a noble civilization or sink into brutality and barbarism. Courage is *not* the feeling of fearlessness. It is rather that willingness of mind necessary to act out of conviction rather than feeling. One may actually feel quite fearless and act in a cowardly manner. Also, one may feel quite fearful and behave with great courage.

Several years ago the wire services carried an account of a printing press operator in the Midwest whose employer signed a contract to print a pornographic magazine. This man refused to operate his press on that one contract. He pleaded, "Allow me to work on any other project. Give me the worst hours in the shop; I won't operate my press when that magazine comes through." He was fired. He appealed to his labor union, which declined to support his "censorship." He lost his job with only three years to go on his pension and retirement.

I discussed this disturbing story with a pastor I know.

"What a jerk!" my preacher friend laughed. "Gagging at gnats and swallowing camels. How big of a deal is it? He doesn't have to read them or look at the pictures. That fool hasn't any responsibility in the matter. All he has to do is operate a printing press."

That pastor's attitude is indicative of a deep wound in our society. When we can no longer even identify which situations demand truly courageous responses, then we no longer know when to take a stand. Finally we will lose our understanding of what courage is. If a society misdefines courage, it is on the verge of barbarism.

THE COST OF COURAGE

Courage is that willingness to deny my own flesh and do what is right and noble, regardless of the cost. I once counseled a young engaged couple who were living together partly because it was financially expedient for them to do so. I counseled them that one or the other of them should move out. I urged that they establish a clean relationship for a full year, to get married only on the solid foundation of a virtuous relationship.

They explained to me how it would be extremely difficult for them financially. I assured them I knew it would take great courage to act virtuously. I was amazed when they accepted my advice.

The expense was not only financial. Their bodies had cultivated an appetite for each other. They were enjoying all the benefits of marriage sexually and none of the responsibilities of the commitment. That is a very difficult thing to reverse, but they did. They acted with tremendous courage, and God blessed them in it.

One of the most satisfying moments of my ministry was receiving a letter from them more than a year later as they honeymooned in Italy.

> Dear Dr. Rutland,
>   This is the greatest moment of our lives because we know that we acted as God wanted us to do. Now we have come on this honeymoon together from the foundation stone of a virtuous relationship. If we had gone on living together and gotten married, we

would only have been asking the church to solemnize what we were already doing. Now we know that our marriage is founded in Christ. We are so happy.

Courage is the first and greatest element of character. Merely knowing what is chaste or honest or true is not enough. It takes courage to act on virtue. Courage is also the catalytic agent that summons every other virtue into action in the face of temptation or crisis.

A contractor agreed to build a house for a certain amount. The contract that called for top-grade materials became unprofitable when a sudden unexpected rise in the cost of materials caught him and many other contractors by surprise. If he fulfilled the contract as signed, he knew he would lose money. He also knew he could use lower grades of materials and get away with it. It probably would not even make much difference in the quality of the house. Now the obvious issue was honesty. He knew the honest thing to do, but his honesty would cost him his profit margin. It required tremendous courage for him to act honestly. Honesty is the virtue resident, but it takes courage to put it into action.

MORE THAN VALOR

Many miss the greater truth of courage by thinking of it solely in terms of bravery. Though bravery may be admirable, courage is far more than valor in the face of danger. Courage and heroism are not exactly synonymous. Acts of heroism may or may not be indicative of true courage.

Heroism in the face of danger may be a momentary burst of instinct not reflective of true character. Some people are simply constitutionally impetuous. They are bolder than others by nature. Sometimes public heroes in war or athletics later live unproductive and even destructive lives. Such people were never truly courageous. They were simply brave.

Imagine two children playing on a swing set. One child,

by nature, loves the thrill of danger. "Swing me higher!" she cries. "Push higher, Daddy!"

It may not indicate any great courage on her part. It may rather be that she has a broad thrill spectrum. Her brother, on the other hand, says, "Not so high, Daddy, not so high." The father thinks the lad cowardly, but in reality he is simply more prudent. To confuse prudence and cowardice is dangerous folly indeed.

"Don't be a coward!" is the stinging rebuke the boy gets for his prudence. His heart is damaged needlessly, for he is not cowardly at all. He may, however, be smarter than his sister.

Furthermore, courage without character can degenerate into mere bravado. The distinction between a hero and an obnoxious show-off is character. In other words, if his motives are selfish and impure, a "hero's" actions may result from a lust for preeminence that overrides good judgment.

Indeed, acts of heroism may sometimes be born of stupidity, ignorance or misunderstanding. For example,while being interviewed by Bill Maher, author Dinesh D'Souza claimed that the 9/11 terrorists were not cowards because they were willing to die.[2] D'Souza was wrong. They were cowards who killed thousands of civilians without warning.

Circumstantial reality may also be mistaken as courage. A condemned prisoner on death row was allowed to select the menu for his last meal. "Mushrooms," he answered. "I want fresh mushrooms. I've wanted them all my life, and I've never tasted them. I've always been afraid I'd get bad ones and be poisoned."

Beyond circumstance, past mere bravery, there is another kind of courage. The courage of true character lifts and ennobles a life. A warrior may fight valiantly, brave all manner of danger, overcome insurmountable odds and defeat a superior enemy, only to plunder the city and outrage its citizenry. Is he courageous? In every classical and biblical sense of virtue the answer is an unqualified *no*. The fearless

warrior who rapes and burns is not courageous. He is a
brute. Courage, true courage, is about valiant goodness.

COURAGE AND PUBLIC TRUST

In the inner office and inner soul of every congressman, our
nation and civilization hang in the balance. Until we can cultivate statesmen who are willing to be turned out of office for
taking a stand for moral issues, a national character will continue to erode.

The congressman who violates his conscience for gain
blasphemes his office and corrupts his own humanity.
Ultimately his character will become so degraded that he
will be unable to take a stand. His vote, his influence and his
soul will cheapen at every resale. Enthroned as an incum-
bent, he may be elected time and again, until he becomes an
empty husk of a politician, but no office gained or kept is
worth the loss of character.

Hardly any endeavor known to man requires more
courage than preaching. The courageous man of God
preaches what is right regardless of whom it pleases or
offends. He not only preaches what is right, but he must
preach what is right in a right way, refusing to compromise
his message or his methods. Likewise, the policeman who
refuses an envelope of money is not only honest; he is courageous. The schoolboy who declines to hear the dirty joke is
not just chaste; he is courageous.

DAILY COURAGE

The long, lingering moral crises of life are the most difficult
and taxing. Those who stand up day after day under with-
ering criticism need a far greater kind of courage than the
once-in-a-lifetime hero. Courage extended in an enduring
crisis is character's most painful and most profound engraver.

A sophomore student athlete at a large university said to
me, "I'm through dating. I've had dates with those I thought

were the nicest girls on this campus. When I did not make sexual advances to them, they made advances to me. And they were aggressive."

He continued, "When some beautiful cheerleader is climbing all over you, begging you for sex, your desires are stirred up. When I refused, they accused me of being a homosexual. Several threatened to tell everyone on campus that I was impotent. The next girl I date is going to be a Spirit-filled, blood-washed daughter of Abraham who looks at this thing exactly as I do, or I don't care if I never date again! I've made my stand on this issue."

The college student needs a durable courage to live out his convictions day after day. He is a truly courageous young man. May God give us more like him.

All hail the professional athlete who plays the Super Bowl in great pain! His is, in a sense, a courageous act. However, he may also be driven by baser motives such as ego and his next contract.

Consider instead the crippled teenager who wakes up every morning in immeasurable pain. She cannot even go to the bathroom alone. Yet every day she sings praises and goes to her job. Day in and day out, she does what she can do with fingers that rebel and a body that screams in agony. She may never be thought beautiful, never be pursued by men, never know the tender embrace of a loving husband and never bear children. Yet day after day after day, despite her pain, she simply does what is right. She is truly courageous, much to be admired. May God give us more like her.

COURAGE AND THE FEAR OF GOD

Fear is not altogether unwholesome. If a man fears the wrong thing, he will probably not fear the right thing. If he fears the right thing enough, he will not fear the wrong thing at all. All lesser fears will be swallowed up in the life of the man who truly fears God.

Proverbs 29:25 says, "The fear of man bringeth a snare: but whoso putteth his trust in the LORD shall be safe."

The fear of man is a trap, but it is harmless and baitless to the man who fears God. The man-fear trap is the leading cause of disease in the development of courage. If we fear God more than we fear the good opinion of our mates at work, our spouses, our congregations or our constituency, we are free. If his ultimate fear is the fear of God, what lesser fear can make a man disobey God's will or deny His name?

The account of Bruce Olson's capture and ultimate release by South American communist guerillas is stirring. It is a study in quiet, beautiful courage. Olson did not overpower his guards or use karate or throw hand grenades. He is a missionary, not John Rambo. In a boldness born of fearing God more than their bullets, he offered to teach them. Most of them were illiterate. He, being a linguist, was more fluent in their Spanish language than they were. Olson offered to teach them to read and write Spanish. They kept him captive until they learned to read.[3] Then they released him. The fear of the Lord makes us calm, quiet and confident.

COURAGE AND LEADERSHIP:
THREE KINGS IN CRISIS

Styles of leadership, in any era, vary widely, but courageous leaders are at a premium in every age. David, Herod and Jesus, all leaders and all kings, are a study in contrasts. Three more disparate kings can hardly be imagined.

Herod was the quintessential tyrant. He was a collaborator as well as a murderous lecher, but the defining crack in his character was cowardice.

David was the consummate warrior king. Larger than history, he lived his life in capital letters. David was like the girl with the curl in the middle of her forehead. When he was good, he was "very, very good, and when he was bad, he was horrid." Yet at many points in his life he showed tremendous courage under extreme pressure.

Jesus, the gentle shepherd, is probably not seen by many as being particularly courageous. He fought no pitched battle, led no troops, scaled no fortress walls; yet, in His ignoble death by execution, we see courage of the highest order.

Scripture affords us a window into the lives of these three kings. By comparing their character under pressures, which is where character is always revealed, we can learn much about courageous and cowardly leadership.

King Herod

King Herod, who had stolen his own brother's wife and was living with her openly, was fearlessly denounced by John the Baptist. Herod himself lacked even the gumption to have the prophet beheaded. He ultimately commanded it because of lust, pride and the fear of looking squeamish in the eyes of his court. When Herod would have executed John, he lacked even the brutal fearlessness to commit murder. Not because he feared God; he feared the people. Fear robbed him of leadership.

> And when he would have put him to death, he feared the multitude, because they counted him [John] as a prophet. But when Herod's birthday was kept, the daughter of Herodias danced before them, and pleased Herod. Whereupon he promised with an oath to give her whatsoever she would ask. And she, being before instructed of her mother, said, Give me here John Baptist's head in a charger. And the king was sorry: nevertheless for the oath's sake, and them which sat with him at meat, he commanded it to be given her. And he sent, and beheaded John in the prison.
>
> —MATTHEW 14:5–10

Fearful of a treacherous woman, a cowardly king killed a courageous prophet. National character is never as fragile as when leaders are more afraid of men than of God. When fearful, blustering, lustful fools lead any nation, its character grows weak indeed.

King David

> And it came to pass, when David and his men were come to Ziklag on the third day, that the Amalekites had invaded the south, and Ziklag, and smitten Ziklag, and burned it with fire; and had taken the women captives, that were therein: they slew not any, either great or small, but carried them away, and went on their way. So David and his men came to the city, and, behold, it was burned with fire; and their wives, and their sons, and their daughters, were taken captives. Then David and the people that were with him lifted up their voice and wept, until they had no more power to weep. And David's two wives were taken captives, Ahinoam the Jezreelitess, and Abigail the wife of Nabal the Carmelite. And David was greatly distressed; for the people spake of stoning him, because the soul of all the people was grieved, every man for his sons and for his daughters: but David encouraged himself in the LORD his God.
>
> —1 SAMUEL 30:1–6

Leadership is a great challenge. The courageous will not shrink from leadership, but when everything goes badly, courage is tested. When "Ziklag" is burned, when their wives and children are carried away captive, the people long to rise up and stone God, with whom they are angry. Instead, they may stone their leader. In the painful loneliness of leadership, unless a man has already developed the ability to "encourage himself in the Lord," his character will fail the test.

David learned to encourage himself in God as a mere youth. When a bear came out of the woods to kill his father's sheep, David said, "In the name of the Lord my God, you won't get these sheep!" He learned to encourage himself in

God when all the other shepherds ran off and left the lambs to the lion. David alone rose up from his sleeping mat and wrestled the lion to the ground and killed it. (See 1 Samuel 17:34–35.)

David said, "God is my strength, and God is my refuge." (See Psalm 46:1.) The Book of Psalms was not written by a man who never knew fear, but by a man who, at times, knew deep and abiding fear. Yet he learned in the face of fear to find ultimate courage in his fear of God. He encouraged himself in the Lord his God.

Amidst the smoldering ruins of Ziklag, men turned their stones in their hands and eyed their leader with cold disdain. The future of civilization in Israel hung by the frail thread of the courage of a shepherd-king. When there is no apparent reason for courage, and God is all that the leader has left, then all he has is everything he needs.

King Jesus

On the night that he was betrayed, his friends asleep in the grass and his enemies within earshot across the narrow Kidron Valley, Jesus fell across a stone in a lonely garden and thought of the impending horror of the cross. Not only the physical agony of crucifixion, but also the spiritual nightmare of God-forsakenness loomed before Him. Some may say He felt no fear. The Bible says that sweat drops like blood splattered on the stone. Fear wrenched in His guts like a knife. Satanic voices screamed in the night. Finally He cried out to God, "O God, I don't want to do this!" It was only when His soul ached for escape and the air was thick with fear that He uttered His great courageous prayer: "Nevertheless not my will, but thine, be done" (Luke 22:42).

Jesus denied the screaming demand of His own will, stifled the tortured cry of His own flesh and rejected fear. He acted in magnificent courage, not awakening His friends, not arming them with swords and not charging across the Kidron Valley to take the city by storm. A cavalry charge might seem manly and brave, but in that moment, for Him, for us, it would not have been courageous.

His enemies came for Him with their torches bright against the night sky and their swords rattling at their sides, and the courageous Savior said, "Here I am; take Me and let these go free." (John 18:8.)

"I don't want to do this."

"I know."

"Please let me stay home with you. Please, Mother, I'll be good."

She could see that his eyes were brimming with tears. Ten is such a tender age, not one at which a boy should have to deal with things like this. His lip trembled, and he clutched at her sleeve.

"It's not a matter of being good, Sean. You're always good. It's about your life. How long can you stay with me? Don't you know that I want you to? I'd love to keep you right beside me all day, every day. That would make me happy, but it would also make me selfish. No, Sean, you have to go back—back to school, back to life."

"I'm afraid." He was so small, so frail and so defenseless against a stupid, cruel world full of stupid, cruel children.

"I know."

"Is it all right? To be afraid, I mean."

"Yes. It's all right."

"I don't want to do this."

"That's all right, too. It's not in the wanting to or in the feeling brave. It's in the doing it anyway."

"Do you think they'll laugh at me?"

She hesitated, wondering how much he could

take from her. "Some will, Sean. Some will stare, others will ask idiotic questions, and some will try to help and be friendly and won't know how."

A sob, a sigh, really, a wet, lonely sigh, deep and full of pain, racked his thin frame. She longed to clutch him to her breast, to protect him from this terrible thing, to drive away and keep driving. She clutched the steering wheel and fought to keep from screaming.

"Do you want me to help you get out?"

"No, they're watching."

"I'm proud of you."

He didn't answer but fumbled instead for the door handle. The car at the curb honked, and she struggled to suppress her rage. What did they want her to do, push him out on his face?

The car door swung open, and Sean hoisted himself out, bracing for a moment on the metal crutches and then hefting his weight up onto the curb. With the left crutch he slammed the door and turned to face the knot of children on the school's front steps. For a moment they stared at each other across the uncrossable gulf of disparate experience—her little son remembering what it was like to have legs, and other people's sons and daughters wondering what it is like not to.

At last, he started toward them, away from her, from the safety of her, swinging his prosthetic legs in syncopation with his crutches.

"I love you," she whispered, knowing he could not hear. "I'm proud of you."

Then the driver behind her honked again, and she shouted at the rearview mirror, "All right, all ready. I'm moving, I'm moving."

CHAPTER 3

LOYALTY:
CHARACTER IN COMMUNITY

～

Only once in American history did the head of state of a foreign government surrender his position and the sovereignty of his own nation to unite with the United States—the Republic of Texas, and its president, Sam Houston.

Adventurer, frontiersman, general and politician, Sam Houston's name was a household word in Texas and in the United States when Abraham Lincoln was an unknown backwoods lawyer. It is fascinating to note that the Texas Declaration of Independence was signed on Houston's forty-third birthday, March 2, 1836. Houston and his army of ragtag volunteers defeated the might of a massive Mexican army and established a fledgling nation whose capital was called Washington-on-the-Brazos. Like George Washington, Houston, the beloved general, became the revered first president of the wild and sprawling new nation of Texas.

Less than thirty years later, Texas, now a state, debated whether to join the Confederacy in secession or to remain with the Union it had voluntarily entered in 1845. The vast majority raucously demanded secession. One voice, Houston's, cried out for national loyalty.

The elder statesman of Texas stumped the state to the point of exhaustion with this message: "The destruction of the

Union would be the destruction of all the states."

Shunned by young hotheads eager for war and dismissed by a new generation, Houston's pleas for national loyalty were ignored. If Texas had listened, tragedy might have been averted. The refusal of Texas to join the Confederacy might well have dissuaded other states, and the bloodiest nightmare in American history might have been avoided. Unfortunately, Houston's cry to remain in the Union was rejected. Houston, now fatigued and discouraged, must have sensed he was failing physically as well as politically.

"I wish if this Union must be dissolved, that its ruins may be the monument of my grave, and the graves of my family. I wish no epitaph to be written to tell that I survived the ruin of this glorious Union."

Pressure mounted on the old warrior to take the oath of allegiance to the Confederacy, but Houston's loyalty held. He refused, knowing that it meant the certain end of his political career in the South and the ostracism of his family. For Houston, loyalty to his nation was stronger than any hope of a political future. He steadfastly refused the oath.

"In the name of the Constitution of Texas, which has been trampled upon, I refuse to take this oath. I love Texas too well to bring civil strife and bloodshed upon her."

He saw the beginning of the bloodshed he prophesied, but he did not survive to see its conclusion. Houston was hurt by the rejection of his leadership, deeply saddened by the horrible Civil War, but unaltered in his devotion to his nation. Sam Houston was a Texan, the Texan, but he was, above all things, a loyal American.[1]

An ounce of loyalty is worth a pound of cleverness.

—ELBERT HUBBARD

L OYALTY IS THE VERY FABRIC of community. Devoid of basic trust in some kind of mutuality of commitment, relationships cannot prosper. Without loyalty, father and son will live as hated strangers, families will disintegrate, and culture will become bestial. Only invented taboos and fearsome superstitions can restrain such a murderous society from utter criminality.

When loyalty is lost, the very fabric of relationship unravels. Even the disloyal depend on someone else's loyalty. The philandering husband will bitterly resent his accountant's embezzlement. The bribed politician howls over his wife's adultery. The issue is not merely hypocrisy; it is a failure to comprehend the very nature of the virtue of loyalty. No one can translate into relationships a virtue that is fundamentally misunderstood. No society can expect loyalty to anchor its relationships once treachery becomes admirable. The seams of community are ripped asunder when treachery becomes an acquired virtue. In a society thus brutalized, no one is safe. Family ties mean little, and friendship means even less. Life without loyalty is fragile in the jungle of betrayal.

If loyalty is understood only in terms of isolated relationships, disillusionment and bitterness are inescapable. That is to say, a disloyal man is disloyal in his character rather than in respect to particular relationships. The prevailing wisdom of contemporary society contends that marital loyalty is irrelevant to job performance.

Quite the contrary! A man is not simply disloyal to his wife; he is disloyal. The wise employer will reason, "If he will be disloyal to his wife, why should I expect loyalty?"

The president of a certain company finally reduced the candidates for a certain opening to two final applicants. Both were very good. In fact, it grieved him not to hire them both. At dinner following the interview, the CEO analyzed the eager young hopefuls across from him.

"Do you mind if I ask a question now?" one of the young men asked. "My wife advised me to get a clear reading on one point, and I really trust her counsel."

The CEO totally ignored the question. Instead he seized the moment to test the other candidate. "What about you? Did your wife send you off with any questions in hand?"

"Hardly," the young man snickered. "She wouldn't know what to ask."

The old businessman chuckled conspiratorially and leaned close, hoping to draw the young man out. "No head for business, eh?"

"No head for much of anything, actually," he answered. "A classic beauty from Boston. As they say, the porch light is on, but nobody is home."

As the two men shared the joke, the boss noticed that the other applicant sipped his coffee and ignored the jest.

"And your wife?" the employer asked the candidate who said he had a question from his wife. "Does she always tell you what to ask?"

"She certainly doesn't control me, if that's what you mean. She is very bright, and I trust her advice in many areas of life. She's really a wonderful person. I wish you could get to know her."

In that one moment the CEO knew he had his man. Someone who will mock his own wife was not for him. Loyalty was clearly in the character of the man he hired, and character was what he wanted.

The moral and social consequences of venerating the wicked are substantial and incredibly shortsighted beyond words. Loyalty is not a matter of trading off. One does not gain six points for voting a straight ticket, then lose three for company disloyalty, finishing at a good, solid plus three. Efforts to isolate or compartmentalize loyalty from the professional aspect of life are misguided and dangerous. A man does not simply act disloyally in some particular arena of his life, unrelated to the rest. A man is either loyal or he is not.

Merritt was a secure, four-term congressman. Only twenty-four hours ago he seemed invincible. Now he held the front page in his hand like a man holding his own death sentence. "Indicted!" the headline screamed. The article went on to outline the charges of influence-peddling and money-laundering. To add insult to injury, his secretary, Margaret, had revealed (along with other things) their long-standing affair in a full-color pictorial spread in *Playboy*. He calmed his jangled nerves and massaged his temples. Don't panic! He was sure he could plea-bargain the charges against him down to a misdemeanor and plead *nolo contendre*, taking a reduced punishment. He must show a sad disappointment with his own humanity but never admit culpability.

Later, in a painfully emotional press conference, he would denounce the newspapers for pouncing on the irrelevant sex scandal. His teary little mouse of a wife would stand bravely at his side while he suffered like a martyr. He played the scene in his mind. "My wife and I have come through this difficult time. We have a new depth

through this incident, and our relationship is
closer now than ever before." At that point he
must embrace her protectively. "We believe the
voters of this district are sophisticated and intelli-
gent enough to separate these personal matters
from my performance as their congressman." He
would then boldly announce his candidacy for
reelection. Oh, sure, many votes would be lost,
but he knew he could count on the evangelical
vote. He was "right" on their issues, and
Christians love to forgive people. In fact, he
would be hailed as a hero by many.

   This was not going to be fun, but he could
make it through. *Life goes on,* he thought.

Loyalty is the willingness, because of relational commitment, to deflect praise, admiration and success onto another.
This loyalty may well be at great personal expense, but it will
edify and bless its object.

   Loyalty never usurps authority. It refuses to accept inappropriate love or praise that might properly exalt another.
Loyalty is the glue that holds relationships together, makes
families functional and armies victorious. Loyalty is the
fabric of society. Without loyalty, no enlisted man can dare
to hope that his general cares whether he lives or dies, and
no captain can expect an inconvenient order to be obeyed.
Without loyalty, marriage becomes a competitive minefield,
companies become dangerously paranoid, and ruthless
power politics will turn bishops into Machiavellian princes.

   Loyalty is the basic element that validates and cements
relationships. If husbands are disloyal to their wives, if children are disloyal to their parents, parents to children,
employees to employers, there is no secure relationship, and
the fabric of community soon unravels.

STOLEN HEARTS

Every month, on a certain day, the king's court in Israel was held for people who had exhausted all possibilities of adjudication in civil and criminal matters. On that day anyone could appeal directly to King David. His decisions, just or otherwise, were final. Of course, the backlog of appeals soon became tremendous.

David's son Absalom exploited this frustration for his own advantage. Standing tall in his fine chariot, the strikingly handsome Absalom created quite a stir. As the resplendent chariot rumbled through Jerusalem, Absalom's youthful good looks and flowing hair were admired by men and desired by women. It became his habit to wait at one of the city gates for those coming on the day of the king's court. Flattered at being summoned into Absalom's chariot, the aggrieved shared openly. He wooed them like a true politician, kissing their babies and consoling their hurts, yet offering no hope that David would prove helpful.

"It's not altogether David's fault," Absalom would explain sarcastically. "He's overworked, to be sure. We all understand that. The problem is that he stubbornly refuses to appoint a deputy. Now if *I* were deputy, or even king, I'd make sure you got justice. The appeal ought to go your way, but with David on the throne, well, who knows?"

No one loves a demagogue like the disgruntled. Grateful malcontents bowed down before Absalom and longed for him to be their champion. Absalom's personal embrace in traditional Middle Eastern style was an act weighted heavily with symbolism. Absalom's familiarity was calculated to seal their loyalty to him personally. Of course, he had no right to such dedication. Only David had a right to that.

> So Absalom stole the hearts of the men of Israel.
>
> —2 SAMUEL 15:6

The throne was Absalom's by birth. It should have and

would have gone to him. His untimely and tragic death, which cost him his destiny, was the inevitable end of his disloyalty and rebellion. His disloyalty caused his rebellion, and his rebellion cost him his life. When outward rebellion occurs, it is always because loyalty was not added to faith.

Loyalty refuses to accept inappropriate credit, receive improper admiration or usurp the respect due others. Such loyalty is usually carved into character at no small cost.

LOYALTY IN ACTION

The pastor of a small Midwestern church announced to his five adult Sunday school teachers, "God has laid on my heart that for the next three months all of you should teach on evangelism. I've prepared these lesson outlines for you. You can adjust them to suit your classes." The next Sunday, all five began the series.

Teacher 1 said to his class, "The pastor said we have to teach this stuff for the next three months. I want you to know that if I were the pastor, we wouldn't teach this, but I'm not the pastor, and this lesson isn't mine."

Teacher 2 obediently taught the material. Her class, responding enthusiastically, actually became soulwinners and caused the class and the church to grow. At the end of the series, they sang her praises. "What a great idea you had to teach this series! What great lessons and marvelous outlines you had!"

"Thank you so very much," she said humbly. "I really prayed over it. I knew God was guiding me as I prepared and taught." Obedient in action, she stole the hearts of the people. It was the pastor's vision, and she should have deflected the praise onto him.

Teacher 3 taught the series of lessons, but it went badly. Everyone in the class ferociously objected, "We don't want to be soulwinners. We like the easy, comfortable Sunday school class we've had for forty years, and you're pushing us out into the streets. We don't want this."

To this the teacher replied, "It wasn't my idea. I never wanted to teach this stuff in the first place! You know how the pastor is. Complain to him." This teacher's unwillingness to shield the pastor is characterless and disloyal.

Teacher 4's Sunday school class also complained to her, but she said, "I felt it was what God was telling me to do. I tried to do my best. If the pastor could only have taught it himself, I know he would have done better. So if you're angry, be angry with me." She loyally accepted the brunt of the criticism, allowing all respect and admiration to pass on to higher authority. Furthermore, she probably told the truth; the pastor would have done better.

Teacher 5's class proclaimed, "This is the most wonderful thing that's ever happened to our Sunday school class!" To which the teacher replied, "I can agree with you because I had nothing to do with it. God and the pastor worked this out. Pastor wrote it and handed it to me. Frankly, I had my misgivings, but I now see that the pastor was right. I thank God that he gave us this series, don't you?" That is loyalty in action.

THE STRATA OF LOYALTY

A particularly ironic confusion arises from our society's general disregard for the virtue of loyalty. We have contracted an inability to prioritize our loyalties. That is to say, confusion in society results from failure to establish appropriate levels of loyalty. Not all loyalties are created equal. Spheres of loyalty will often conflict. Weakness and instability in character will be the result of failure to distinguish levels of loyalty and to resolve this inner conflict.

A double-minded man is unstable in all his ways.
—JAMES 1:8

Only by working downward from the ultimate loyalty can such dissonance be avoided. By first establishing the nonnegotiable, which can never be denied, the tension is eased at descending levels. Once that loyalty among all loyalties is settled, questions of conflict are more easily resolved.

A woman came to me for counseling claiming that her husband was ordering her to engage in prostitution. He was not a Christian, but he knew she was. He made this perverted demand by exploiting her convictions. He was head of the household, and she must be loyal to him. She evidently had accepted some kind of strong, legalistic teaching that convinced her that, no matter what her husband said, she had to submit to him as head of their household. This Christian woman was actually considering acceding to his demands.

She was deceived by confused loyalties combined with a false sense of submission. By allowing a secondary loyalty to her husband to supersede her ultimate loyalty to Jesus Christ, she nearly entered into serious immorality. Her unsaved husband was using her slavish misunderstanding of Scripture to manipulate her into doing what he wanted.

Another woman with whom I once counseled was awaiting her criminal trial for embezzlement. She had gotten involved with a man who was heavily in debt. He had pleaded with her to get some money for him or he would go to prison. She embezzled a substantial amount of money from her job to help him, fully intending to repay it. The scandal of her arrest was a bitter shock to her church and her family. When I asked how she could have fallen for such a tired old line, she responded that "she had no idea."

She was right! She had no idea. She rationalized her disloyalty to her God and to her employer by hiding behind loyalty to a man, and not much of a man, at that.

MARRIAGE: OUR COVENANT OF LOYALTY

For the married, loyalty to spouse is second only to loyalty to God. A marriage can struggle along racked by bitterness and unforgiveness, but once the cracks of disloyalty appear, only the grace of God can save it.

My wife and I have counseled with many couples whose marriages have been shaken by extramarital affairs. We try to bring them to the point of being honest with each other about the adultery. In so doing, we have found that husbands and wives generally ask very different questions.

Betrayed husbands typically ask questions about the sex. "Was he a better lover than I am? Was there something he did for you that I didn't? Did you enjoy him more than me?" Wounded wives more frequently ask, "Did you talk about me with her?" That shocked me the first time a woman asked it. I thought to myself, *Of all things, that's what you want to know? You want to know what he was talking about?* Her husband was sleeping with another woman, and she's interested in what they talked about! I came to realize why the wives and not the husbands were asking the truly important question. The wives wanted to discern what the act of immorality really meant. They intuitively grasped that in the pillow talk the true depth of the disloyalty could be discerned.

Loyalty in marriage is quite the same as loyalty in any other relationship. It means constantly building up the other, even at one's own risk or expense. I cannot imagine a woman being more loyal to her husband than my wife is to me. When I go to preach where my wife has previously spoken, I am often asked, "Are you really as wonderful as your wife says?" Of course, that makes me feel like a million dollars. I must, of course, humbly defer to my wife's wisdom and discernment.

Her loyalty, in turn, makes me want to respond in kind. It escalates, and we begin to race with each other to see who can build up the other more. For many couples the same cycle seems to work in reverse. My wife and I are always shocked to hear couples argue and contradict each other in public.

The husband will say, "I remember back in 1957, we moved to Topeka."

"No, no, dummy," the wife interrupts. "It was 1956."

"No," he insists, "it was 1957 because it was the year Charlie was born."

"Great!" she cries. "That's typical! It *was* the year that Charlie was born, but he was born in '56. You don't know any of the birthdays of the children."

This tedious argument goes agonizingly on and on until I imagine myself jumping on the table like the Mad Hatter, stamping about in the tea cakes shouting, "I don't care! I don't care whether it was in '56 or '57. And I don't care about Charlie's birthday!"

Such pathetic arguments are a complete breakdown of marital loyalty. The loyal wife allows her chronically confused husband to state categorically that it was 1957 even if she knows it was actually before the Crimean War. Alone in the car, away from everyone else, she tenderly reminds him, "I know you said 1957, and you're probably right. You almost always are. It just seems to me we were driving a DeSoto that year. Did we own a DeSoto as late as '57?"

That affords him a little latitude. If she shouts "1956!" like the volcano goddess, he is going to fight back. It is naive, if not insane, to think he is going to admit in front of five other couples, "Oh, yes, dear, you're right. What a donkey I am."

Husbands, on the other hand, often say the most outrageously disloyal things disguised as jokes. "Are you going to eat *all* of that?" the husband asks as his wife's banana split arrives, borne by two waiters.

Her spine rigid with wounded, feminine pride, she announces, "Yes, I'm going to eat this and five more. By Christmas I intend to be as big as the Hindenburg."

A small gathering at our house was attended by a couple who were desperately trying to dig their way out of debt. The woman loudly complained *ad nauseum* that her husband had taken a second job. The family never saw him, the children were neglected and she felt like a widow.

When my wife suggested that the woman help her in the kitchen for a few minutes, they were gone for nearly half an hour. When the woman came back, she looked like a naughty child returning to class from the principal's office. For a while she sat quietly. Then, completely out of nowhere, having nothing to do with the conversation, she announced, "That reminds me of what a wonderful man my husband is! Did you know he has taken a second job? He works so hard just to take care of me and the kids."

Alison had helped her realize she was being disloyal to her husband. She was tearing her husband down in front of others, which in turn elevated her stock with no one.

THE DISLOYALTY OF CRITICISM

In criticizing the wisdom and ability of a superior, a subordinate lowers himself. Logic dictates that the lesser works for the greater. Therefore if the boss is the champion nitwit of all time, what kind of people would work for him? If the boss is an all-around great person of tremendous insight and wisdom, the happy conclusion is that surely he showed wisdom in his hiring decisions. When I lift up my boss, I am lifted up. When I brag on my wife, I shall be held in honor by others. If I speak of her disloyally, others will agree with me that she certainly is stupid, stupid enough to marry me! Likewise, if my parents are the village idiots, well, they raised me.

VERTICAL LOYALTY: A TWO-WAY STREET

Loyalty must function both upwardly and downwardly. Upward loyalty is shown to our superiors. It is being willing for them to get the credit while we take the blame. This is the key to corporate loyalty. If the middle-level employee, with subordinates beneath him and superiors above him, shows any disloyalty, the fabric of community in that corporate structure begins to shred.

The CEO of every corporation should periodically invite

someone to teach his employees about corporate loyalty. They must know how to deflect praise and admiration onto the boss while being willing to accept the blame when things go badly.

I have sometimes had the unfortunate experience of calling someone's office only to have a secretary say, "I don't know where he is. Many times he doesn't even come in until 10 or 11 o'clock. I guess he's playing golf somewhere."

That is a blatant disloyalty, a deliberate attempt by that secretary to make her boss look bad. Perhaps it is an attempt to convey that she is working while the boss plays. It may also be an effort to prove her own value. Perhaps she is saying, "I don't know what my boss would do without me."

Upward loyalty helps to fulfill the superior's dreams. Lower-level managers are generally not hired to be visionaries. Any institution must operate on only one vision. An obvious example of this is an ambassador. Ambassadors do not get paid to have opinions, but to clearly communicate for the head of state. When a U.S. ambassador presents himself to a foreign government, no one there cares much about the ambassador's ideas. They only want to know what the president thinks.

DOWNWARD LOYALTY

Some time ago I went to a certain place of business owned by a man named John. I was there to meet him and several others for lunch. As we waited for our last arrival out in John's reception area, we chatted amiably with John's private secretary, a receptionist and a junior executive. Finally the last of our party arrived, quite late. As he rushed into John's reception area he apologized, "I'm sorry I'm late. My secretary didn't show up, and everything's crazy at my office. I'm having a terrible time with my staff."

John, in whose office we stood, said, "I know exactly how you feel. The worst thing I face is getting good help!" He said this in front of his own staff! I was so surprised that I couldn't keep from looking at his employees' faces. They looked as though they had been slapped. The younger associate literally slumped, and his secretary spun on her heel, went into her office and closed the door rather too loudly. The receptionist sat down and started pounding her keyboard like Lizzie Borden. I searched John's face for some sign of hostility, and, finding none, I realized that he was not being cruel but insensitive. He had no idea what he had done.

As soon as John and I were alone, I said, "Brother, do you realize you just lacerated three of your employees? You badly hurt your own stock with those people." He was genuinely surprised, but when I rehearsed the scenario for him, the light gradually dawned. I said, "Think about how you would feel if that had happened to you. Your employees felt betrayed. You were disloyal to them. Furthermore, you missed a golden opportunity to strengthen their loyalty to you."

Downward loyalty happens as people at the top say, "I couldn't get this done without my employees."

Bosses should constantly be saying, "Our success is largely due to my great team of associates." They should be praising their employees, not just to their faces, but to other people.

THE SUPERNATURAL POWER OF LOYALTY

The redemptive grace of loyalty is so powerful it can literally infuse any situation with healing and miraculous blessings. Any force that powerful, however, cannot be violated without dire consequences. There are few virtues in the kingdom more honored by God than loyalty. Absalom's doom was sealed by his disloyalty to David, but David's loyalty to an unworthy Saul confirmed his destiny for the throne.

In the household of Naaman, a Syrian general, there lived

a young Jewish slave girl. She had been captured by a Syrian raiding party. Plucked from the bosom of her family, alone in a foreign land, she served as a personal body slave to Naaman's wife, hardly a circumstance to inspire loyalty. Even the most outwardly obedient slave might murder his master mentally. Yet this little girl chose to be loyal with her whole heart. Somehow her family in Israel had deeply instilled loyalty in her character at a tender age. Now a slave in Syria, her well-shaped character found genuine concern for the one who owned her just as he owned his horse.

When Naaman contracted leprosy, the slave girl told her mistress, "Would God my lord were with the prophet [Elisha] that is in Samaria! for he would recover him of his leprosy" (2 Kings 5:3).

Amazing! She sent him who held her captive to her home country, where she surely longed to be. She sent him to be set free of his disease, though he held her in slavery. She genuinely wanted Naaman to be healed, and he was. The miracle that Naaman received by the ministry of Elisha never would have happened without that slave girl's unlikely loyalty.

Grateful for the miraculous healing, Naaman offered Elisha a substantial reward, which Elisha declined. Elisha's servant and understudy, Gehazi, shook his head in amazement. The Syrian had been miraculously healed! *Why shouldn't Elisha be blessed?* Gehazi reasoned in his heart. *Do not muzzle the ox*, he thought to himself.

Elisha refused the luxurious gifts of the Syrian, but Gehazi would not. He waited until Naaman was out of Elisha's sight, and then he raced after the foreign general. Elisha had changed his mind, Gehazi explained to the Syrian. Two visiting prophets had arrived, and Elisha would now be happy to accept some gifts after all. Naaman was only too delighted to give.

Elisha, however, discerned the deception and struck the hapless Gehazi with leprosy. In other words, if Gehazi wanted the Syrian's money, then by all means he should have the Syrian's disease as well.

The greed of Gehazi is obvious. The subtler issue of disloyalty is more easily overlooked. For personal gain he misrepresented his employer's motives. Acting out of self-interest, he denied his superior's nobility, goals, purpose and will. What an ironic contrast!

A slave girl's character and loyalty brought miraculous healing and blessing, while the disloyalty of a prophet in training brought scandal, disease and death. Loyalty is a gemstone virtue whose luster, in a golden setting of faithfulness, brings glory to God and health to all it touches.

CHAPTER 4

Diligence:
Character in Action

≈

The sickly, squalling slave baby was handed over to one of the elderly women. No one—not the plantation owner, Mr. Moses Carver, not the slave woman in whose arms he screamed—no one saw any hope for the child. What hope could there be for George Washington Carver, an African American baby born in the waning days of the Civil War and orphaned when his father died and his mother was kidnapped by slave-stealers?

The frail lad's earliest years were spent in poor physical health, but he was mentally and spiritually strong. There was no school for African Americans in Diamond Grove, Missouri, but the young boy learned to read on his own. Hours spent, at his own initiative, mastering spelling, grammar and syntax reaped a great reward. By age ten, George Carver was moving from town to town seeking out anyone who would feed his ravenous appetite for knowledge.

When, at the age of sixteen, George Carver became the first African American admitted to Iowa A & M, (now Iowa State University), his early education was the fruit of diligent self-application. Excellent marks, a winsome personality and a commitment to servant-leadership made him an academic and social success at college. After graduate school he became the first African American admitted to Iowa A & M's faculty.

Carver subsequently left Iowa to join Booker T. Washington at Tuskegee Institute, where he found international fame for his work in agricultural research. It was not his scholarship alone, however, that endeared him to his students, his colleagues and the world. Carver's unflagging commitment to excellence, to diligently see the job finished and finished right was the foundation upon which he built a life of worth.

Born a slave and an orphan, George Washington Carver proved that character can lift a life above its beginnings. He was a man of diligence who could not be defeated by a whole world of obstacles.[1]

Diligence in employments of less consequence is the most successful introduction to greater enterprises.

—SIR FRANCIS DRAKE

THIS A PERVERSE SOCIETY INDEED that lauds its occasional genius and scorns the diligent. How strange that we so honor the gifted, who are what they are without effort or sacrifice. What honor is due them?

Western civilization has placed a premium on talent while quaint relics like diligence gather dust in the moral flea markets of our age. In so doing we cultivate characterlessness. The modern American sees work as the curse of the masses. The faithful, diligent journeyman is mocked as an unimaginative peon unworthy to be in the same room with the fey royalty of creative genius, even if that genius is corrupt, base, unproductive and undisciplined. The hard working and the disciplined often go unrewarded while temperamental and characterless "geniuses" are elevated.

American industry is rapidly gaining a reputation for creative ideas that will not work and a lazy, undisciplined work force that cannot produce. American industry is confused by its own mythology. We have been taught that, despite slipshod methods, disregard for diligence and short-run, quick-fix tactics, American ingenuity will somehow make it all come together at the last minute.

We stare disillusioned at vehicles that will not run, savings and loans that fail, ministries that do not last and companies that go bankrupt. In the 1950s, American industry laughed at pitiful Japanese efforts to mimic the West. With classical

Oriental diligence they set to work. Creative research and development, they said, will come. Later we will innovate, but first, they maintained, we must work. They proved to be true what we once knew: Genius is a fragile substitute for character.

Likewise, American education has squandered its soul and its power in a philosophical vanity fair. We are now reaping the bitter harvest of a generation of fanciful but quite useless theory. Our schools and universities continue to spew out graduates who can explain the peyote cult and do African folk dances but cannot hold down jobs. The university campus, we are told by undisciplined dilettantes, is to be the marketplace of ideas. What about the idea that diligence is not the last resort of the boring and unimaginative? Diligence is the virtue that leads on to balanced, successful living and creativity unfettered by dissipation and decadence. Theory is no substitute for practice, and creativity without character will quickly corrupt.

Stories such as the one about the tortoise and the hare must appear laughable antiques to the modern student. The diligent tortoise now plays comic straight man in an educational system that celebrates the madcap talent of the hare and blames his ultimate failure on a society unable to accept a genius ahead of his time.

When a class is studying Edgar Allan Poe's brooding prose, why not teach the young to learn from his destruction and get a heart of wisdom? In addition to reveling in Poe's works, we must lament the unwritten stories washed away by booze. Instead of producing young musicians who have merely mastered Mozart's concertos, can we no longer marry character to genius so as to defeat Mozart's demons? The genius of Mozart must be recognized. His pathetic waste is a cautionary tale to the wise. While studying the art of Van Gogh, we must dare to speculate on masterpieces never painted because of dissipation. Diligence is the virtue that sets us free to fulfill our creative destiny.

DILIGENCE AS STEADY APPLICATION

Steady application may not necessarily elevate the peaks of the super performer, but it can put a foundation under him to minimize the depth of his valleys. Furthermore, it enables "Steady Freddy" to reach his potential. The diligent man is a steady performer, and the steady performer is a *finisher*.

One of the most frequent weaknesses among the immature is a will-o'-the-wisp lightheartedness about obligations. For example, it is not uncommon for an otherwise serious Christian to testify glowingly, "I was supposed to go to work tonight, but I just felt the Holy Spirit telling me to be here at Bible study." That direction did not come from the Holy Ghost. Don't blame irresponsibility on God. The deceitful heart, absent character, would rather enjoy the fellowship at Bible study than bag groceries.

Well-meaning zealots may say, "I am called to missions. I know I'm supposed to give two weeks' notice, I also owe some money, and my dad co-signed on my car, but God is telling me to go into the mission field—right now!"

No, He is not! God is calling all of us to be diligent, faithful finishers. If we cannot be trusted to pay our debts, how can He trust us to save Africa?

For good or ill, we always impact with our own character those things committed to us. As we are engraved with the image of Christ, all those areas in which we have stewardship must also bear the stamp of His character.

DILIGENCE AS IMMEDIATE OBEDIENCE

Diligence not only finishes the job, but it does so without unnecessary delay. Paul called it "being instant" (2 Tim. 4:2).

It is a true character-shaping virtue to do it now. Procrastination is not merely an inborn personality weakness. Procrastination is a sin and a sign of spiritual backsliding. The diligent have disciplined themselves to hear from authority and obey now. Hence, when God speaks, the diligent are the very ones who hear from God and obey now. Children must be taught that if they cannot obey parents whom they can see, they will never learn to obey God, whom they cannot see.

There is another and even more ominous danger in procrastination. As we procrastinate, we begin to believe that God also is a procrastinator. The Word of God teaches that God who is faithful will execute judgment in His own time. When it happens, it will come suddenly. We dare not project our slackness on God. The downward cycle of life in a society without diligence is grim. Because authority is not diligent to punish, lack of diligence is learned. A generation with no fear of authority becomes less diligent. Indolence and idleness breed sin and rebellion, but authority lacks the steel to be diligent in punishment. To such a people, the wrath of God seems unrealistic, if not laughable, and, at the very least, avoidable.

DILIGENCE AS EXACTITUDE

Ezra 7:23 says, "Whatsoever is commanded by the God of heaven, let it be diligently ["exactly," ASV] done for the house of the God of heaven: for why should there be wrath against the realm of the king and his sons?"

In other words, do it now, do it exactly as instructed and do it until it is finished. America's romance with creative individualism has often worked to a disadvantage in this regard. The free-thinking lone wolf is often celebrated while the obedient and diligent are mocked.

I took a young man on a mission trip to Peru some years ago. We were going into the Amazon jungle to Puerto Bermudez. I had been there many times and knew the journey well. By rented car we would go from Lima to La Oroya; from there to Tarma and finally to La Merced. It would be a long, cold, dangerous night's journey. From La Merced, by an ancient bus, we would travel down into the jungle town of Puerto Bermudez. I knew it would take more than twenty-five hours from Lima. It is a frightening, excruciatingly tedious journey. I knew we would arrive at a lonely jungle army garrison at about three in the morning. I did not think I had to explain to my companion, a young man in his twenties, all the reasons for my instructions.

I simply said, "Now look, put your passport in your shirt pocket. Keep it there, and put everything else in your suitcase."

When we arrived at the military checkpoint at three o'clock in the morning, everyone was nervous and irritable. Peru is an immensely dangerous place. People are being killed every day. The soldiers are nervous. The people are nervous. There is nothing scarier than ten or twenty nervous, tired soldiers manning a jungle outpost at three o'clock in the morning. They are scared of you. You are scared of them. The whole situation is nerve-racking.

When we jolted to a stop, I awakened my young friend. "Come on," I said. "Get out of the bus."

Everyone on the bus shuffled into line in front of a captain seated at a desk. Sleepy soldiers guarded the line with machine guns. The captain began checking and stamping travel documents.

"What are they doing here?" asked the boy.

"They're going to stamp our passports. Get yours out," I said.

"Passport?" he asked, with horror in his voice. "It's in my suitcase."

"In your suitcase?" I demanded. "Do you mean the one tied on the top of the bus, underneath that goat?"

"Yes," he whined, "up there."

I calmly explained the situation to him. "In a minute that man over there will demand to see your passport. When you fail to produce one, those soldiers will point their machine guns at you. At that time I'm going to step away from you."

He begged pitifully, "Dr. Rutland, please."

"I told you to put your passport in your pocket," I said.

Then he said those hated words. "But I thought…" he moaned. "I thought it would be safer up there."

"Yes," I said, "but you did *not* do what you were told. Now *you* would be safer up there."

At that very moment the sullen captain muttered, "*Pasaporte*." His voice shaking, my young friend said, "I don't have it," and began gesturing at the decrepit bus. When I saw three Uzis trained on him, I quickly stepped away.

We had to get the goats off the roof of the bus. We had to drag the suitcase down. We had to go through it until we found his passport. Everybody on the bus was angry at us. They were literally cursing us. Finally we had to repack his suitcase, lift it back on the top of the bus and replace the goats. When we finally rolled out of the outpost, it was five o'clock in the morning. What should have taken us fifteen minutes took nearly two hours. The soldiers were angry, people were angry and I was angry. Why? Because of three fatal words: "But I thought…" Ingenuity has its place, but the greater virtue is diligence, in this case coupled with obedience.

One concept that the immature have difficulty grasping is that doing a secular job well, exactly as instructed, has an enduring spiritual impact on character. There is a connection between the way I do my job or clean my room and my relationship with God. If I do the things required of me in a resentful and rebellious manner, diligence is not being carved into my character. The task may get completed, but my character remains untouched. When anybody believes that diligence in worldly matters is of no spiritual value, his own spirit suffers.

Negative spiritual lessons are learned when obedience and diligence are held to be unimportant. When God calls on the man without diligence, he will prove unfit. He may delay. He may do it halfway. He may improvise. Eventually, however, he will fail the test. Partial obedience is disobedience.

Delayed obedience is disobedience.

Character does it promptly. Character does it exactly as told. Character finishes it.

DILIGENCE AS CAREFULNESS

To be diligent also means to use care. For example, the young stock clerk is told, "Stack these five boxes." He may do it quickly and complete the task, yet fail utterly by breaking everything in the boxes. In this sense, diligence has to do with attitude as well as action. We must do every job as unto the Lord. I must make my job as important to me as it is to my employer, or I sin against him.

Throughout the time I was in college, my wife and I worked hard to hold body and soul together. I often worked at two or three jobs doing whatever I could do to raise the next semester's tuition. At one job in a grocery store, there were also two other guys who worked there. One was a hotshot local basketball star. His coach had arranged for him to get the job there in order to pick up some spending money. He thought it was a lark, so he played at the job. The other fellow, Tom, was a slightly retarded young man. The basketball player constantly made Tom the butt of every joke. Yet I learned much by watching that mentally retarded boy bag groceries. Whether there was one person or fifty persons in line, he never altered his course. He would carefully place one can at a time in the sack, not allowing pressure to force him into error. He never hurried. He never got flustered. He never tried to move faster than he could do the job efficiently.

The basketball player was six-foot-nine and marvelously coordinated. When he wanted to, he could bag groceries like a whirlwind. With one hand he could bag groceries faster than Tom could with both hands at top speed. Then the athlete would start clowning or be in the back taking a break when he was supposed to be bagging groceries. Worse still, he was rude to the boss and to customers. I have seldom been as delighted as I was to watch as the manager fired that basketball star. He fired him right in front of us all, including Tom. I will never forget that manager pointing his finger at the retarded boy and telling that basketball star, "You see this kid? You don't think much of him, do you? He is worth his weight in gold, and you're not worth a dime."

I learned a character lesson in that grocery store. Just be the best you can be. Just put the groceries in the bag one can at a time. Just finish. Just do it right. Just do it with care. Tom cared about the job. He wanted to do it right. He felt a responsibility to the grocery store. He handled a can of tomatoes as if it were a live baby. The basketball player dropped crates and burst open boxes. He deserved to be fired.

Diligence is also important in relationships. We must be sensitive to others, aware of what is going on around us. The husband who forgets his wife's birthday is not simply stupid. He is not diligent before God. An apology the day after her birthday is not worth a hill of beans. The damage has been done.

Why do American teens feel so little spontaneous impulse to help? A mother, carrying two bags of groceries and a gallon of milk as she struggles with the door, calls out, "Somebody come and help me." Her great big teenage boy will casually get up off the couch, lay the funny papers aside and reluctantly lumber over to hold the door for her. Why doesn't he jump up and carry the bags without being told? It is because he has never been taught to open his eyes and look at her. He does not really see what she is doing.

The diligent who learn to be observant of others seldom have to apologize later for being thoughtless.

DILIGENCE IN MINISTRY

Characterlessness in ministry is particularly harmful. There is something arrogant about spoiled ministers who do not seek to be aware of what God is doing. Such failure even to attempt to be spiritually alert to the situation is sinful and self-indulgent. Asleep at their posts, lacking in prayer, not diligent in the Word, they cannot, with any confidence at all, say, "Thus saith the Lord." Spiritual diligence, to hear and obey God, is one absolutely essential ingredient in a ministry of genuine power.

OBSERVANT IN BUSINESS

Diligence also means to be on guard, careful, watching over the situation as if it were your own. It means to limit disruptions and distractions.

Secretaries can pay attention to each other, or they can be attentive to duty, to their employer and to the situation. The diligent learn to sort through information and see what is worthy of attention. Those clustering around the proverbial water cooler are neither discerning nor diligent. There is some information that is totally useless. Listen with discernment, and limit time spent on useless information.

DILIGENCE AND TEMPTATION

The diligent will also be stronger in the face of those surprise temptations that arise suddenly to defeat so many. Everyone will be caught unaware from time to time, but those who are diligent in the things of the world tend toward diligence in the things of the Spirit. The lion is not nearly so able to leap out from hiding and destroy the diligent with unexpected temptations.

Recently I counseled a young man whose girlfriend was pregnant. He said, "We never intended this to happen."

Of course, he never intended it! That, however, was the very cause of the problem. The young couple was not intentional. They did not intend to sin; they were swept into it by passion. The lack of intentionality caused them to be caught in a situation where they failed morally. Through lack of diligence, sin became inevitable. Biology is a tremendous force.

We must teach our teens to show their respect for its power and with due diligence.

A Christian who reads the Bible and prays every day, necking passionately in the back seat of a car, is no safer than an unbeliever in the same situation. At some point, all that awakened passion steals all ability to stop. Once the point of no return is passed, sin is inevitable. Look ahead at the situation. Be observant to possible danger, and avoid it.

I have been all around the world and have seen all kinds of things. I have never heard of anybody getting pregnant in a prayer meeting. We often drift into sin because of simply not being observant. Round and round the mulberry bush, the monkey chased the weasel. The monkey thought it was all in fun. Pop goes the weasel! A diligent monkey does not chase lethal weasels. He is alert to the danger in the situation.

DILIGENCE: KEY TO GROWTH

None of this is to glorify self-will. Self-discipline is not a way to sanctify ourselves. God must do that. Still, we cannot go on worshiping our own bellies while praying to God to add virtue to our lives. God expects us to discipline ourselves.

A.W. Tozer said, "We have been snared in the coils of spurious logic which insists that if we have found God, we need no more seek Him."[2] Only by having met the Lord can we realize what it really means to seek His face diligently.

Diligence is a key to prosperous, successful living in temporal matters, but God uses temporal concerns to teach spiritual lessons.

WHAT DILIGENCE IS NOT

Diligence is not driven, anxiety-ridden, burdened perfectionism. That neurotic lifestyle finally becomes temporary and counterproductive. The driven, perfectionistic workaholic, always unable to reach his own unattainable standards, is obsessed but not controlled. He loses his awareness of reality and of the people around him. His wife, children and the real circumstance of his own health and limitations are ignored. He is neither prudent nor cautious. He believes himself to be diligent about work, but in reality he has his nose buried in his own obsession. Do not confuse drivenness with diligence. Diligence is productive and enduring.

THE FOUR FACES OF DILIGENCE

The virtue of diligence has four faces:

1. Diligence means *constancy*. Temporary obedience is disobedience.

2. Diligence is *instant*. Delayed obedience is disobedience.

3. Diligence is *exactitude*. Partial obedience is disobedience.

4. Diligence is *observant care*. Careless obedience is disobedience.

Diligence is the responsible, orderly, steady application of God's power within me toward whatever responsibility is mine.

DILIGENCE AND COMMITMENT

The Latin form of the word *diligence* is *diligentia*. It derives from two root words that mean "to choose" and "to love earnestly." The diligent, therefore, can make and be faithful to a choice, even one that is contrary to the immediate demands of the flesh.

In marriage, therefore, the diligent husband knows that true love transcends the emotional rush of the honeymoon. Love is constantly choosing. The diligent love earnestly because they choose to love, and they choose to love no matter what. There is a dreadful fragility in any marriage that depends on love being "felt." There will be those moments in any marriage, or in any relationship, when honeymoon romance is nowhere to be found. In those seasons we must love not passionately but earnestly, because we choose to do so.

Diligence makes all of life a labor of love, all the way to the finish line.

Mountain High School's battered old Blue Bird bus was symbolic of the track team it carried. The ancient vehicle seemed to be held together with wire. It was not pretty, and it looked like a relic from another era, but it ran fairly well and got where it was supposed to go.

Bouncing along on the torn green seats inside, the little team attempted in vain to act confident and relaxed. On the front seat, gruff old Coach Hardeman pretended to be dozing. His hat was shoved forward over his eyes, and his arms were folded across his chest. Mr. Wheelwright, the good-natured school janitor who doubled as the bus driver and campus Grandpa, whistled the same nondescript tune he had been whistling for years.

The boys were mostly quiet except for the occasional outburst when a spit-wad SCUD found its mark or when some halfhearted insult earned reaction. They were intimidated. In fact, they were terrified. Never in Mountain High's inglorious athletic history had any of its teams made it to the state meet. Many of the boys had never seen Lexington. Blue Rock, Kentucky, seemed insignificant to them as they stared out at the huge city. It made them feel insignificant as well. Despite the forced joviality, several wished they had not come.

Suddenly Coach Hardeman sat up straight, pushed back his hat and stretched his arms above his head. Spinning to face the boys, he stared down the length of the shabby old bus. He searched the face of each of his skinny charges.

"This here's a big city, ain't it?" he asked.

The boys muttered their assent, staring vacantly out the windows.

"I don't reckon we gonna win every event," he continued. "But no school in the state is gonna win 'em all. The main thing is, you're here! This is an invitational, and you were all invited. You deserve to be here."

"We'll do our best, Coach," Donny shouted.

"Yeah, I know you will." The coach smiled as he spoke.

"Coach, what about the long-distance race?" Harold asked. "Craig's home with the mumps." This last comment, which was a fact everyone knew, brought forth a burst of laughter.

"I'm glad you asked that, Harold, because I have a surprise for everyone. Beau is going to run it."

All eyes turned to the face of the senior water boy. Year after year Beau went out for the track team only to be made the manager. Beau grinned sheepishly from the back seat and shrugged his shoulders.

"But, Coach…" Cass objected.

"No buts! All of you have your own events. I asked him, and he agreed. That's that." Coach set his lips in a firm line.

From the back, somebody muttered, "He can't win. Heck, he can't even place high."

"I didn't ask him to win or place high. I only

asked him to finish," Coach answered as little
Beau, water boy, turned to gaze without expression at the passing traffic.

The day went pretty much as expected.
Mountain High placed third in the 100-yard dash
and fourth in the 440 relay. That was it. As they
began repacking their gear, they heard the top-ten
finishers in the long distance race being
announced as they crossed the line.

Out of a statewide field of one hundred run-
ners, finishing tenth was an accomplishment. But
Beau's name was not among the ten.

The lights began to dim as the last of the spectators drifted toward the parking lot. The
Mountain High boys stared in confusion at Coach
Hardeman. He was gesturing madly at the head
official. The two men's voices were loud, nearly to
shouting, but the boys could not hear the words.
The rugged mob of Appalachian teens drifted
closer to the argument.

"All right!" they heard the official shout. "We'll
turn the lights back on. But it makes no sense.
The track meet's over. Just call him in."

"No," Hardeman said. "I told him to finish. Let
him finish."

"All right, all right," the official muttered. "Turn
'em on," he shouted up to the control tower by the
press box. "Turn the lights back on!"

Only when the stadium lights came back to full
power did they see him. Struggling around the far
turn was Beau. His arms dangled limply at his
sides. His frail legs barely moved. The boy's head
wobbled pitiably.

They stared at him in incredulity. The return of
lights drew the attention of the few remaining

spectators loitering at the gates, and they began
drifting back toward the infield. The lone figure
laboring up the cinder track moved toward the
finish line in obvious agony. Gasping for breath,
the boy struggled with each step.

As the cluster of spectators grew, the Mountain
High track team became aware of the comments
of the adults around them.

"Look at that."

"Why doesn't he quit?"

"I never saw anything like it."

Suddenly somebody cheered. More cheers.
Oblivious to the rising cheers, Beau Rogers tried
to concentrate on nothing but the finish line. His
legs were screaming in pain. He knew he was close
to vomiting. Still he came. Right. Left. Right. Left.

He collapsed across the finish line and into his
coach's arms. The team swarmed around him,
shouting and jumping on him as if he had just
won an Olympic gold medal. As the boy lay back
against Coach Hardeman's arm, he became aware
of the excitement around him.

"What are they cheering about, Coach?" he
whispered.

"They're cheering for you, son. They're
cheering you."

It made no sense to the boy. What did it mean?

"I finished, Coach, just like you said," he
answered.

"Yeah, Beau, that's right."

CHAPTER 5

MODESTY:
CHARACTER AS SIMPLICITY

∽

"How's your boy, Bob?" asks the tall, slim man in the plaid shirt.

"Fine, Mr. Blanchard," answers a burly truck driver with a day's growth of beard. *"He took a turn for the good last week."*

"Well, we're praying."

There is nothing unusual or spectacular about the brief conversation in the graveled parking lot of a Christian men's retreat in South Georgia. Two men—regular guys, a businessman and a truck driver—exchange greetings and prayerful concerns with the casual ease of equals and fellow travelers. Nothing exceptional. Nothing at all, until you realize that "Mr. Blanchard" is James H. Blanchard, CEO and chairman of the board of Synovus.

Phenomenally successful in business and extremely influential in politics, Blanchard disdains any hint of flamboyance and extravagance. Approachable, humble and a fiercely dedicated Christian, James Blanchard lives where he was born, in Columbus, Georgia. He has resisted calls to move Synovus (a banking credit card empire worth more than $20 billion) to New York. *"Columbus is home,"* he says, in his soft aristocratic Southern drawl, as if that explains everything.

Now able to take his place among America's most successful businessmen, James Blanchard remains unimpressed with himself. As comfortable on a bass lake as he is in a boardroom, more concerned with a truck driver's son than he is with the stock market, James Blanchard's modesty has endeared him to the locals.

A convenience store owner in Columbus said of the banking magnate, "Blanchard is real people."

That is perhaps the highest compliment for a truly modest man. Blanchard, while quietly comfortable with his own success, walks in cool balance falling neither to prideful self-promotion nor to that particularly nauseating false humility of the inwardly arrogant.

He just is who he is, a successful man, blessed of God, using the resources at his command for God and for good. Resisting the flashy flamboyance of many less wealthy than himself, Blanchard walks in authentic modesty.[1]

Nothing can atone for the lack of modesty; without which beauty is ungraceful and wit detestable.

—SIR RICHARD STEELE

THE EARLY CHRISTIAN COMMUNITY WAS Jewish. Its struggle was not to know how to live a holy life. Since remotest antiquity, the Law of Moses had prescribed the tiniest details of family, business and social life. The struggle for those early Jewish Christians was to comprehend salvation by faith in the gracious Messiah. As they met on Solomon's porch, early Messianic Jews were not seeking a radical change in lifestyle. They were celebrating the love and liberty of the Holy Spirit while awaiting the return of the King.

However, as Jesus delayed His return, Jewish Christianity was forced out of the temple, out of Jerusalem and finally out of Israel. Gradually the Christian movement began to puncture the soft underbelly of the Greco-Roman world. The insularity of Jerusalem hardly prepared them for the jaded decadence of the decaying remnants of imperial glory. Rome had become a tired old whore whose depraved appetites corrupted not only its flamboyant royalty, but also the general population as well. Dry rot had reached the courts, businesses, theaters and the families of the Roman world.

In the blazing revivalism of Ephesus (Acts 19), the impact of Christianity was an immediate change in lifestyle. Huge collections of magic books and paraphernalia were burned. The Ephesians were idolatrous Gentiles, not legalistic Jews. Their idols, mostly silver statues of the goddess Diana, were destroyed, and they refused to purchase more. The silver-smiths who made the statues knew that this new lifestyle for the Christians meant an end to their industry, and riot resulted.

In Jerusalem, however, no bonfires of the Torah were burnt. There was no particular industry that depended upon pervasive sin. Christianity was a theological issue in Jerusalem. In Ephesus, Corinth and Rome itself, the question was how to live as a Christian in the putrid atmosphere of decaying paganism.

Christians in Jerusalem in A.D. 33 were asking, "When will He come again, and what will the restoration of David's kingdom look like?"

Christians at Ephesus less than thirty years later were asking an entirely different set of questions: "How do we do business? Should we buy meat dedicated to pagan gods? How should we treat slaves? How should our women dress?"

By the late nineteenth and early twentieth centuries, Western civilization had been Christianized. Certainly that does not mean everyone was a Christian. It means rather that the mores, values and ways of living were profoundly informed by Christianity.

Not everyone was honest, but there was a societal consensus about what honesty was. Not everyone went to church, but going to church was considered a "good" thing to do. Likewise, not everyone was modest, but modesty was considered a virtue.

That's not necessarily true anymore. Modesty is now more often considered the neurotic repression of both sexuality and individuality. In fact, many reason that if America is about individual liberty, modesty may actually be "bad." Part of the problem the church faces today is that, in addition to being misunderstood, modesty has often been applied narrowly by the church itself. Now we are in the post-Christian era of the West. The moral decay around us is forcing

Christians to come up with answers that are no longer "givens." Fending off the old legalism of Jerusalem on the one hand, we must also resist libertine corruption on the other. In many ways we are headed back to Ephesus.

LIVING WITHIN LIMITS

Most modern Americans understand the word *modesty* to have reference only to one's manner of dress, and even then it is mostly used with regard to women. Yet modesty actually has far more to do with self-respect and self-control than with how revealing one's garments are. Style of dress is an application of modesty, not a definition.

Modesty, in its classical sense, means living within limits. Modesty submits to the boundaries of propriety. It is the opposite of being "bold-eyed," putting oneself forward in the sense of being overly aggressive or presumptuous. Modesty has to do with being other than boastful and arrogant.

Modesty springs from a tempered and humble estimation of one's own importance. It is unobtrusive, but it is not bashful. Modesty acknowledges the fact that there are limits of propriety on life and that it is good to submit to those. Modesty sees restraints as being positive safeguards, not negative hindrances.

Immodesty denies responsibility to law, culture, authority and tradition. Immodesty is personally offended by signs that say "Keep Off the Grass." Modesty says, "There are things in this world that are right for me to do and things in this world that are not right for me to do. I am not too good, too big, too rich or too powerful for someone else to point those out to me."

Modesty is not mindless subjection to authoritarianism. It is rather the conviction that there are correct limits on life. In addition, the modest learn to set their own limits. Modesty has a great deal to do with one's self-view.

There is a great insight on modesty in Romans 12:1–3:

> I beseech you therefore, brethren, by the mercies of
> God, that ye present your bodies a living sacrifice,
> holy, acceptable unto God, which is your reasonable
> service. And be not conformed to this world: but be
> ye transformed by the renewing of your mind, that
> ye may prove what is that good, and acceptable, and
> perfect, will of God. For I say, through the grace
> given unto me, to every man that is among you, not
> to think of himself more highly than he ought to
> think…

That is the essence of modesty. That passage was written
to help pagans in ancient Rome and modern America understand that modesty means much more than how a woman
dresses.

Paul says, "I beseech you therefore, brethren, that ye
present your bodies a living sacrifice, holy, acceptable unto
God" (Rom. 12:1). Obviously, then, we are precious. We are
important to God. Otherwise the sacrifice of our lives would
be totally unacceptable to Him. If your body is a sacrifice
that is acceptable to God, then treating your body with
respect is also important to God.

Verse 3 says, "Do not think of yourself more highly than
you ought" (NIV).

In other words, a sacrifice is acceptable to God only as
long as it is on the altar. When it is presented unto God, it
finds its meaning. Withdrawn from the altar of God and
reclaimed in arrogant, presumptuous self-ownership, your
body loses its meaning and therefore its value.

Hence, in being yielded as a sacrifice under the ownership
and lordship of Jesus Christ, I find meaning and explanation.
When I take my body and my life in my own hands, I make
myself meaningless and valueless; my life becomes an
unending search for ways to convince myself and the world
of my significance.

Modesty is unassuming and genuinely humble. The immodest announce by demeanor, dress and attitude, to everyone in general and to the opposite sex in particular, "Look at me. I am what is important in this place."

As she passed the full-length mirror, Kristy checked herself out. She was transfixed by what she saw. She was very pretty, if not actually beautiful. Even better than beautiful, however, Kristy was rich and beautiful.

Her hair was exactly as she wanted it, though she complained about it constantly. Her sweater-shirt was obviously expensive and fashionable. The top two buttons were open, and the braided gold chain that delicately graced her smooth neck lay across her upper chest. From the chain dangled a seven-hundred-dollar cross with a beautiful little diamond. Her father had complained that it was too expensive for a teenager's necklace, but her mother had successfully interceded as usual. After all, a girl's sixteenth birthday comes only once. It wasn't as if her father could not afford it.

Kristy opened the sweater's third button, revealing a shapely figure. The teenager knotted her brow, wrinkled her nose and pursed her lips in the cute pout with which she consistently charmed most males and many females. She rebuttoned the sweater, pouted again and finally unbuttoned it yet again and pulled the sides open just a tiny bit more.

The cross looked absolutely tantalizing on her upper chest. There, that was better. Anyway, the

cross should show. It was a birthday present. After
all, it was a cross, and everybody in town knew her
family was very prominent at First Church. She
was not ashamed of that. She tossed her head,
corrected her posture and swirled from the
mirror, out of the girls' bathroom and into the
lonely hall.

A few quick strides later Kristy stood at the
door of the yearbook office. The rest of the com-
mittee was inside. She knew they had already
been working for three quarters of an hour and
were likely to be unreasonable with her. She
would fix that. With her hand on the doorknob,
she carefully arranged her most dazzling smile,
absolutely confident of its effect.

She threw open the door and danced in, non-
chalantly tossing her purse onto a nearby desk.

"Sorry I'm late," she sang out to the room in
general.

"What else is new?" answered Carl "the Nerd."

She flashed him her most wounded look but
said nothing, waiting for others to try to make her
feel better. They did not. Instead, the six other
teenagers continued their work with hardly a
notice of her presence.

"Hi, Kristy," said Elizabeth, the yearbook
editor. A chorus of half a dozen "hellos" followed,
but they were shockingly halfhearted. Kristy
seethed at being so blatantly ignored. Were they
trying to punish her for being late?

"Well, I see I'm not needed," Kristy muttered
petulantly.

"Sure you are," Elizabeth said patiently.
"There's enough work for all of us. Why not trim
those pictures on that desk?"

"OK," Kristy answered quietly. She really did not like Elizabeth. Elizabeth was pretty in a way, but she just did so little with herself. Elizabeth was what Kristy's father called a "real little lady." The phrase made Kristy sick, but she felt she should be seen with Elizabeth occasionally. That girl was well-liked and extremely smart.

Kristy ambled over to the desk littered with pictures, sat down and listlessly began the required trimming. She had learned over the years that being barefooted in a room full of people with shoes on always got attention. She thought it made her look free and uninhibited. She lifted both feet and let her pumps drop to the tile floor with a very satisfying clatter. At the noise, several boys glanced at Kristy. Now Kristy studiously ignored them.

She propped her feet on a chair and lounged backward, pretending to be absorbed in the scissor work. She knew she was finally starting to get some attention. Sitting like that with her feet up, more of her legs would be exposed. Well, who cares? She was just being herself. Could she help it if they looked?

Kristy knew her father would not have liked it. If he could see her now, he would fume just as he did whenever she wore shorts to night church. He was sweet, but he was also completely out of it, she thought. In a few minutes three of the boys were at her desk, and Elizabeth, Carl "the Nerd" and that Vietnamese girl were working alone at the other.

Kristy's father wanted her to be more like Elizabeth. No, thank you! Anyway, Kristy was a Christian girl. Her father ought to be happy. She

wasn't taking dope. She just didn't let musty old
rules get in the way of her happiness. After all,
"where the Spirit of the Lord is, there is liberty."
That was the motto verse for her youth group,
and she liked it.

    Kristy glanced at Elizabeth there at the editor's
desk. The girl sat quietly, earnestly doing her
work. Oh, Elizabeth was just a bore. Worse than
that, Kristy knew that for some unknown reason
Elizabeth disapproved of her. How could that be?
Kristy was one of the nicest girls in the school.

MODESTY AND CONTROLLED LIVING

Modesty also keeps its emotions under appropriate control.
There is an emotional immodesty that indulges itself in
extravagant displays of emotion. To the emotionally
immodest, their every tragedy is the worst thing that has
ever happened to anybody. Where a balanced person may be
mildly happy, the immodest are careening off the walls.
Emotions need expression, but the acceptance of limits is the
key to balance. There are certain limits outside of which the
expression of emotions is improper and even dangerous.
Modesty has no inordinate need for attention, because of a
calm self-acceptance and self-possession. Modern
Americans, for example, have made heroes out of bragging,
extravagant, arrogant athletes. In victory, excruciatingly
boring, in defeat, sullen and graceless, they reveal, on the
field and in their lives, a character untouched by modesty.

    Modesty teaches that it is not necessary for a
thirteen-year-old boy to enter every room like an entire
roller derby team. Boys must be taught that doors need not
be kicked open. On the other hand, we dare not squelch
their childlike enthusiasm for life. Modesty is not passionless

living. It is passion under control; it is passion that accepts the limits of propriety.

We usually think of modesty mainly in connection with clothing and fashion. It is uselessly legalistic to ask such questions as how short is too short and how sheer is too sheer. The more important questions about modest dress have to do with being showy or inappropriately seeking attention. Immodesty may have as much to do with excessiveness as with brazenness. In that sense, then, one might have an immodest hairstyle that is excessive and flamboyant and demands attention.

Modesty that is fastidious and judgmental will become legalistic to say the least. It is false modesty that nitpicks and criticizes youthful enthusiasm and discourages joy and vitality. Such pharisaism is hateful and binds people up.

GUIDELINES TO MODESTY

Many Christian ask what styles of dress, makeup and hair are acceptable, but listing is petty, soon dated and may miss the point entirely. On the other hand, some guidelines to modesty may be helpful.

- ◆ Always be suspicious of the flamboyant. Remember that you are trying to express the orderly, decent, modest glory of God through the way you dress.

- ◆ Instantly suspect fads.

- ◆ In clothing, particularly, try to avoid those styles that are provocative and draw attention to your body.

Now again it must be stated that there is a balance. Holiness does not always have to look like it has been thrown away. We have been through that in generations past. The point is that an inner conviction to seek modesty requires Christians to look in the mirror and honestly ask themselves some searching questions: Are these clothes just slightly too tight? Is this dress just a little too low cut? Will these clothes be an unnecessary temptation to others?

Modesty is the quiet, dignified celebration of the sacredness of one's privacy with God. Recently a young actress explained her nudity in a movie by asking, "Well, what about Adam and Eve? They were naked in the Garden of Eden. I'm not ashamed of my body either."

What about Adam and Eve? In the first place, they did not even know they were naked. What a wonderful innocence that must have been. If you can return to that, then you only have to deal with one other fact. There are six billion other people who are certainly not that innocent. Furthermore, that which is used for a shameful purpose becomes shameful, and that which is used to incite lust or cause guilt in others is shameful. The body is not shameful and should not be used shamefully.

Of her short skirt, a woman said, "Well, my legs are my best feature, and I'm going to show them off." Without realizing it, she is asking for the rejection of herself as a person. She will never feel good about herself as a person, and she will not appreciate her true worth if she feels valued only for her legs.

God is for the body. The body is holy, a living sacrifice, acceptable unto God. Modesty does not want to inspire the unhealthy attention of others. It does not want to be the center of attention. Modesty—true, balanced, wholesome modesty—wants Jesus to be the center of attention.

It is perfectly reasonable for a Christian woman to look in a mirror and ask herself, "Could I do with less makeup?" No woman is going to go to hell because of makeup. Even so, a modest woman learns to ask herself, "How can I use makeup within the limits of propriety?"

The modest man learns to look in the mirror and ask himself some questions as well: "Do I feel comfortable with myself, and is God glorified with this attire?" A Christian man need not ooze worldliness. Let him search his heart first, then his wardrobe and jewelry.

It is *not* legalistic and pharisaical for a teenage boy to look at himself in the mirror and say, "Now that I'm saved and filled with the Holy Spirit, I want to serve God. I have always worn my blue jeans so tight they looked as if they were spray-painted on. Do I have to go on wearing them like that?" It is *not* too much to expect that he reinspect his entire wardrobe and hairstyle in search of a more modest, restrained, controlled way of living.

It would be easy if the "Ninety-seven Rules From God About Modesty" were to descend from heaven. That is what the Pharisees thought they had. They were wrong and, in their wrongness, became legalistic and hateful. Their modesty was as fleshly as the prostitute's immodesty. There are no rules like that because God will not give them. Instead, we must make decisions about makeup, clothing, attire and all related matters because our hearts are His home and our bodies are a living sacrifice to Him.

CHAPTER 6

FRUGALITY:
CHARACTER AND PROSPERITY

When Oseola McCarty was in the sixth grade, she dropped out of elementary school to become the principal care giver for her dying aunt. She never returned to school, working instead doing laundry and ironing for Hattiesburg, Mississippi's aristocracy. In 1920, a twelve-year-old African American with a sixth-grade education had little to look forward to but hard work.

Oseola McCarty turned her life of service into an anthem to character. Caring for her aunt, then her grand-mother, and finally her mother, Oseola became the family hospice. She supported herself and her relatives with her work as a cook and domestic and, in the process, earned herself a public reputation as trustworthy, loyal and diligent.

In private, except where no one except some local bankers could see, Oseola McCarty was carving into her youthful character a strength that was eventually to benefit many. Year after year, for more than seven decades, she lived and learned true frugality even on her marginal income. Living at what some would call a poverty level, she still saved. In local banks, buying CDs, setting aside the small but regular deposits, Oseola McCarty found herself, at the age of eighty-eight, prepared and empowered to do grandly what she had done her whole life.

In July 1995, a humble washerwoman who never attended junior high school presented the University of Southern Mississippi with a check for $150,000. An endowed scholarship for minority students now helps others to an education she never received.

A stunned USM administrator said, "This is by far the largest gift ever given to USM by an African American. We are overwhelmed and humbled by what she has done."

A life of character—a humble, hardworking, sacrificial life built on the conviction that servanthood is noble and important—now enables a new generation to find success through education. The character of Oseola McCarty, however, is her most enduring contribution. Out of a lifetime of laundry, sometimes earning only a dollar a bundle, Oseola McCarty, in quiet character, earned and served, and saved that others might receive.[1]

Frugality is founded on the principle that all riches have limits.

—BURKE

WHEN A SOCIETY DROPS FRUGALITY out of its moral hardware, the national character begins to twist like sheet metal in a blast furnace. Frugality is that virtue the absence of which touches the very substance of life, and poverty of every kind will follow. Indeed, it will be even worse than that. A society without frugality loses its capacity to evaluate what is really precious.

If the base, the precious and the semi-precious all look alike to a society, it becomes impossible to discern the difference between humanity and plastic, between life and a bauble. A society is defined by what it wastes as well as by what it wants.

The toothless hag was terrifying to look at. Duan-pit stared at the fearsome old woman and felt hot tears flood her eyes. The tears began to trace wet streaks down her smooth eleven-year-old cheeks. They dripped onto her bright native shirt. The chubby-faced little girl made no effort to hide or stem her tears. She did not even lift her little brown hands and wipe them away.

Her mother tried to comfort her, but what comfort could she give? Duan-pit knew that the wretched-looking old creature was buying her from her father. The old procurer carefully counted baht into her father's eager palm. It was a great deal of money for a man as poor as her father.

Duan-pit did not know what would happen to her in Bangkok. Other girls from her mountain tribe had been sold into the whorehouses. She knew that. She had heard the adults talk about it. What she did not know was exactly what a brothel was.

She was terrified, confused and hopeless. Sobs began to rack her body like the uncontrollable shakes of malaria. The old woman triumphantly laid the last baht into her father's outstretched hand. That hand quickly closed around the wrinkled, colored money with a finality that made Duan-pit scream.

A few minutes later Duan-pit's father watched as the woman walked briskly down the winding jungle trail. At the end of a rope, following her like a lamb, walked his youngest daughter, her tiny hands bound behind her back. The old woman totally ignored the child's pitiable howls.

Now, the man said to himself, he could finally get that new radio he had wanted for so long. In fact, the stupid old witch had paid so much he could get a case of beer, some cigarettes and a lantern as well as the radio.

He watched the girl a while longer, then turned back toward his hut. He fingered the roll of bills in the pocket of his shorts. Of course, he hated to see the girl go, but what is a girl compared to a radio?

FRUGAL OR STINGY

It is difficult to teach frugality to postmoderns because the very word has utterly disappeared from their functional vocabulary. Among those in whose vocabulary it does remain, there is a great deal of confusion about what it really means.

Many identify frugality as mere thriftiness, but the thrifty can easily become stingy, then loveless, judgmental and withholding. Stinginess separates us from those who look to us for providential care. Sometimes, wise parents learn, it is better to buy the double-dip ice cream cone, even though the child will never finish both dips. Fiscal responsibility knows that the second dip is a waste of money, but sometimes love must be the law. Frugality springs from a balanced view of things and life. Stinginess may actually be a lack of frugality. What passes for frugality is sometimes only an obsession with smallness and pettiness.

I had a friend in college, Dennis, who prided himself on being frugal. Actually, he was dangerously obsessed with money. I remember the great issue of shoelaces in our sophomore year. Before it was over, I was quite sick of Dennis and his shoelaces. He broke a shoelace, and it became a federal case. He complained for two weeks, not so much because the shoelace had broken, since he had worn it for years and thought it was about time for it to break, but because he could only find shoelaces for sale in pairs. This he resented bitterly. How he moaned, "I don't need two. I only need one." He blamed the entire American industrial system for selling shoelaces only in pairs. That is not frugality, and it is not a virtue. It is an obsession with pettiness, and God hates petty living.

A certain Scotsman was traveling on an English train. When the conductor came to collect his ticket, the Scotsman complained about the fare. "I refuse to pay it. It costs too much."

The exasperated conductor asked, "What do you mean, it

costs too much? That's the announced price. If you don't buy a ticket, you'll be put off."

"I want you to cut the cost in half," whined the Scot.

They argued until the frustrated English conductor finally shouted, "I'll fix you." Just as the train went over a high trestle above a river, the English conductor threw the Scotsman's suitcase out the window.

The Scotsman screamed, "What's the matter with you, man? You not only want to steal my money, but now you've drowned my only son!"

False frugality always sees itself as acting virtuously by doing things that are irrational and unethical. Penny-wise and dollar-poor can become a way of life that destroys homes, relationships and businesses.

Stinginess can also become judgmental toward what it perceives to be the excesses of others. A frugal lifestyle is a virtue, but the law of love must preside over our attitudes toward the possessions of others. In other words, God may give another liberty at one level regarding possessions that He does not give me. I have neither the right nor the discernment to decide what God is saying to another. Legalistic judgments about others will make me presumptuous and condescending. Law separates people. Frugality is not about imposing laws on each other, but is rather about hearing from God for ourselves. Frugality is character's attempt to cultivate a lifestyle pleasing in His sight and effective in our pursuit of both holiness and prosperity.

TRUE FRUGALITY

To speak of being frugal implies far more than saving money. Frugality is not the opposite of generosity. It is rather the opposite of reckless wastefulness. Frugality, like modesty, has to do with controlled living. The great point of frugality concerns the purpose of things. Frugality is not so much a question of how many things I own but of their purpose and place in my life.

There is, for example, a purpose for leisure in life. Recreation is to rebuild, to re-*create*. It has a function in life. Everyone needs times to recuperate from stress and fatigue. We need times when we do something just for the fun of it, just to relax and have a good time. When frugality is lost, however, recreation gets out of balance.

In one church I pastored, there was a well-to-do couple. The Sunday they left for a trip to the South, we said good-bye to them after the morning church service. That night they were back in the evening service.

"Did you change your mind?" I asked.

"Well, the air conditioning was broken on the car, and we couldn't stand it with the windows rolled up," they answered.

"Well, why didn't you just drive with the windows down and have the air conditioner repaired after you arrived?" I asked in hopeless naiveté.

"Are you joking?" the lady asked in a shocked tone. "Drive with the windows down? People might think we couldn't afford air conditioning."

They actually delayed their vacation rather than ride with their windows down because they were afraid people would think they could not afford air conditioning.

Consumption without frugality produces an escalating cycle of things without purpose. Thus the power of mammon eats into our lifestyle and our character.

Frugality, true frugality, is not about buying non-air-conditioned cars (even if you could find such a thing). It is rather about understanding the connection, the dangerous link between things and my view of life, value and others.

FRUGALITY AND MONEY

I remember a certain chap I ran into on an airplane coming out of Los Angeles. As he flopped into the seat beside me, it was obvious he was terribly irritated. Before I could even introduce myself, he announced, "The first thing I want you to know is I never ride coach. My travel agent took care of this. They're always supposed to book me in first class. I admit I didn't check my ticket, but I got here, and the first-class section was full. They've stuck me in coach! I just want you to know I don't travel coach."

Christians often struggle with the wrong question. They ask, Is the added comfort worth the added cost of first class? That misses the point. It may be more frugal to travel first class under certain circumstances. The issue is not money but attitude. It is useless to debate whether or not traveling first class is a sin because it costs more. If I cannot afford to travel coach because I am afraid that people will think I am the kind of bloke who cannot afford first class, then first class is for me a sin. It is a sin, and only by deliberately, intentionally depriving myself of it will I ever master it.

Richard Foster says, "Money is not something that is morally neutral, a resource to be used in good or bad ways, depending solely upon our attitude toward it."[2]

This is a bit too mystical and brooding for me, but his warning must be heeded. A rather more balanced view is that of John Wesley, who said, "Money is an excellent gift of God if it is used excellently, answering the noblest needs of humanity."[3] To Wesley, you see, money was not the enemy. The enemy is my own sinful nature. Therefore, in order to arrive at a balanced view of money, I must ask myself frugality's simple questions.

What is money for?

Money is for exchange. Money is for goods and services that may, without corrupting my spirit, add education, comfort and beauty to my life and to the lives of those I love. Furthermore, money is for the good of humanity and the expansion of the kingdom. Money is never to be used for the purchase of status. Neither is it to be used for the demonstration of power.

Richard Foster used an excellent example of how the misuse of wealth corrupts. In a brilliant parable out of his own childhood, Foster reports that he was a champion marble shooter. They played for keeps, and he was the best in the whole neighborhood. Finally, none of the kids had any marbles left because Richard Foster had won them all.

In order to display his wealth and power, he carried his hard-won fortune out to the pond and, while the other children watched, meticulously threw the marbles in the water. It was a cruel, ruthless and vicious demonstration of power and wealth.[4] Foster also reported that it was a dark and evil moment in his childhood.

James, in his epistle, talks about the way we treat the wealthy in church. (See James 2:1–9.) Money often speaks in church, and it does not always say, "Praise the Lord." Wealthier men frequently have more to say about the spiritual conduct of the ministry. If I need advice on the business aspect of the church, I surely want to find that advice and counsel from those who seem to know something about it. I am far more likely to take advice about business from those who have succeeded than from those who have not. When it comes to the spiritual dynamic of the church, however, we dare not be cowed by those who hold the purse strings.

Who's in charge here?

Am I controlling money, or is it controlling me? When ethical decisions are based on the bottom line of finances, money is in control. Are we making our decisions according to God or mammon? Man cannot serve two masters at one time. He will always love one and hate the other. Financial expediency corrupts faith like demonic rust and eats away at character, destroying submission to authority, humility, obedience, holiness and patience.

Money must never control us. We must control it. I do not believe there is some mystical, evil power inherent in the dollar bill. What I do believe is that there is a weakness in my own flesh. Therefore I must humble myself under the hand of God. I must show mammon who is in charge here. It is the Lord Jesus Christ—not mammon.

Will I let character set the limits?

Am I willing for God to limit aspects of my life through a commitment to frugal living? In other words, when there is not sufficient money for me to pursue a certain course of action, am I willing to believe that it is not God's will for me to do it now? We easily confess that the positive abundance of funds can be used by God to affirm a course of action. If that is true, the contrary may also be true. From time to time God may pull tight the purse strings in order to stop me from a course that is not in His will. Therefore, lack of funds may be a way that God can use my commitment to frugal, modest living to keep me from continuing in a path that is wrong for me.

Frugality is the willingness to endure limits on myself. A grave danger inherent in the American credit system is that it allows me to consume at a level of superficial prosperity, which is not based on any real wealth. Sooner or later, of course, the piper must be paid. Bankruptcy in America comes dressed in a tuxedo, not in rags. Fooled by their own mirage of wealth, Americans are amazed when financial disaster hits them.

I find it difficult to discover a vocabulary sufficient to express to modern Westerners that it is possible to do without some things. My wife, Alison, and I once shared a weekend retreat with some young couples. We told them that we got married when we were nineteen and seventeen years old. I asked, "Do you realize we were married three years before we ever bought a car?"

Utterly uncomprehending, they asked, "What do you mean, you didn't have a car?"

I said, "I'm trying to tell you. We didn't own an automobile."

They gaped at me like modern children quizzically inspecting some ancient agricultural implement.

"We just don't know what you're talking about. How did you get around?"

I said, "I walked. I hitchhiked to school. I hitchhiked home. I hitchhiked to my first job. At midnight when that one was over, I hitchhiked to my second job. I rode the bus."

"Rode the bus?" they marveled.

Provoked by their astonishment, I plunged on. "Do you realize," I said, "that we were, likewise, married for three years before we owned a couch? We had an old army cot on which my wife arranged folded quilts so it looked flat. She made a little coverlet that lay across it and hung to the floor. It looked vaguely reminiscent of a couch, but it was an army cot. If anybody came to visit, we would caution them, 'No, don't sit on the couch.' If they came in too fast and sat on it, the pitiful contraption would shoot out from the wall, hurling their legs in the air like a carnival ride."

The young couples could not get enough of this rhyme of an ancient mariner.

"Why?" they asked. "Why didn't you buy a car and couch?"

"We couldn't afford it," I said.

"What do you mean, you couldn't afford it?" they asked. "Why didn't you just charge it?"

I realized then that we were speaking completely different languages.

We must again master the primeval art of waiting on things until we can pay for them. Credit can be a good thing, but its misuse destroys character. It creates a mirage of prosperity, becoming a self-made sword of Damocles. Cars, houses, furniture and clothing dangle dangerously above the heads of the indebted. If they have no real wealth, sooner or later the whole bundle will fall.

FRUGALITY AND ARROGANCE

Frugality finally wrestles with an even deeper question. Not only am I willing to live as I can afford to, but am I willing to live on less than I can afford? For the sake of self-discipline or simply because it is not a wise expenditure, there are times to forgo even that which I can afford.

It is a sinful arrogance indeed to assume that since I have ten million dollars, I can afford to use even one dollar to light cigars. I can *never* afford to do that. The exercise of that kind of carnal abuse of finances will destroy character. The abuse of money to demonstrate power and express conspicuous affluence gives no glory to God, and it helps no one. It is wrong to burn money on the end of a cigar when people are starving to death.

FRUGALITY AND REPENTANCE

To see financial restitution as a proper use of money is unfamiliar to modern Westerners, but it was not alien to the ancient Jew.

Jesus looked up into the tree and called out to Zacchaeus, "Come down, little fellow. I'm going to have lunch with you."

The man's response was immediate. Zacchaeus said, "I've cheated the poor. I confess."

Just like that! He confessed, "I'm a cheat." He went on to say, "Here's what I'm going to do, Lord. I'm going to give half of all that I have to the poor. To everyone I've cheated, I will pay them back four times."

Jesus perceived that Zacchaeus's entire attitude toward money had changed. Money no longer had a hold on the little man. The power of mammon was broken, right there on that limb.

Jesus said, "Salvation has come to this house today." (See Luke 19:1–10.) The word that Jesus used might well be translated *deliverance*. Jesus announced, "This man has been delivered, and his whole household has been set free from the controlling power of mammon." Zacchaeus proved Jesus right through his new and proper use of money.

In other words, if I have cheated anyone, frugality demands that I pay it back. If I owe anyone money, I will make it my goal to repay the debt. If I have withheld my tithe, I must now give it and more, much more! I must give until I am free.

THE PLACE OF PROSPERITY

If I live a frugal life with a balanced view of money, what about prosperity in my life? I think the church has often failed to communicate a balanced view of prosperity. On the one hand there are the hyperspiritual who say money is altogether evil. Get it away from you. Give it away. Do not have anything to do with it. It is nasty, dirty and filthy, and it has a spirit in it that will get you. Then let there come a need to pay for something in the church, and they will ask folks to give money. You see, having told them how bad it is, they now ask God to give the congregation enough of it to support the church.

On the other hand, others say that God is a God of riches. God wants to bless you, they reason, and if you are right with God, you are going to be rich. Therefore, if you are not rich, it must be because you are not right with God. Stranded in between these two extremes is the great body of people who are living day-to-day on the money that they can earn while trying to provide for their families and improve their lives. What can we say to them? There is nothing inherently evil about needing or having the finances to get by in this life. John Wesley had a magnificent equation for this. He said to earn all you can. Earn it righteously. Earn it in a way that brings no shame to people and no shame to God. Earn all you can.

Second, save all you can. Now, saving all you can does not

mean hoarding it. It means setting limits on my lifestyle in order that more might be made available to the kingdom of God and not go up in the smoke of mere consumerism. Saving all you can is crucial to frugality.

Earn all you can. Save all you can. Then Wesley adds the missing element: Give all you can. Frugality saves to give. Greed gives to get. Frugality plots and plans, schemes and denies self, and sacrifices in order to give more next year than this year.

I want to suggest that you have a family meeting. Ask yourselves, "What can we do to give more than we gave last year? Is there any way we can live a more modest life, something we can do without, some excess we can lay aside in order that we may make a greater investment in the kingdom of God than we have ever made?" I believe that is pleasing to God. It will engage your family's attention for the things of the kingdom and draw their eyes away from the power of mammon.

CHARACTER: FREE TO BE FRUGAL

Frugality is the strength of character that will set us free from the terrible grip of mammon. It may not be immorality that finally erodes our national character. It may be the price of designer tennis shoes. The prosperity of God is a great blessing, a dangerous one, but a great one. If greatly used, prosperity can do much good. Hoarded or squandered, it corrupts character and destroys families. Oseola McCarty had it right. Work hard, serve folks joyfully, save frugally and give generously.

CHAPTER 7

HONESTY:
CHARACTER AND TRUTH

When the German battleship Ostfriesland was sunk by bombs dropped from an American airplane, the career of General Billy Mitchell sank with it. The top brass in the post—World War I American army saw airplanes as high-tech gadgets whose expense was prohibitive and whose only purpose was battlefield reconnaissance. Mitchell, the commandant of the Army Air Corps in WWI, saw the future and dared to tell the truth. The next war, he said, would depend on air power. His counsel rejected, Mitchell arranged for a public exhibition of that power. General Pershing and other WWI generals said it was impossible to sink a battleship from the air. It took Mitchell twenty minutes.

Mitchell's loyalty, prophetic foresight, genuine patriotism and zeal for the truth earned him a court martial. Convicted of insubordination, branded a crackpot and drummed out of the army he loved, Mitchell never backed down. He simply told the army and the country the truth.

Much of the nation and some in Congress listened, but the generals hated him and commanded him to be silent. He refused and continued lecturing and writing. In 1923, he was reduced in rank, and in 1925, despite a public outcry, he was court-martialed and suspended without pay.

The court martial of General Billy Mitchell was an attempt to silence the truth, a truth that might have saved American lives and altered the course of history. His offense was telling the truth, and telling it with stunning accuracy. His analysis that Pearl Harbor was virtually defenseless to air attack from Japan was labeled as hair-brained and politically insensitive. His prediction that the Japanese would someday land paratroopers in Alaska was mocked and rejected as an attempt to gain support for an American paratroop corps that he advocated. Because leadership, rigidly and selfishly entrenched in old paradigms, rejected that truth, Mitchell paid a heavy price for his honesty. Though a hero to some, he was a "renegade" to others, a rebel whose name was a joke in the highest echelons of the military.

In 1936 he wrote, "All of the people who sat on my court martial will be leading the forces defending our country in the Second World War. I hope someday they will be honest enough to admit they were wrong." He further wrote, "World War II will commence within five years." He died that same year with an estate worth a grand total of $5,000. He lost everything because he told the truth. Mitchell did not live to see it, but the Japanese did bomb Pearl Harbor and did, in fact, land paratroopers in Alaska. World War II commenced within the five years he predicted, and the officers on his court martial, including Douglas MacArthur, led the American forces.

In 1946, the army and the nation formally apologized to a man committed to telling the truth regardless of the cost. General Billy Mitchell was posthumously awarded the Congressional Medal of Honor.[1]

The best measure of a man's honesty isn't his income tax return. It's the zero adjust on his bathroom scale.

—ARTHUR C. CLARKE

IN THE EARLY 1970S I ministered occasionally in the federal penitentiary at Atlanta. I have no idea whether I helped anyone on those visits, but I know they were a constant source of education to me.

One man I met there was named Eugene. He had embezzled hundreds of thousands of dollars from a corporation that sold infant products. Yet he complained bitterly that a country music artist had stolen a song he composed. Eugene made a clear distinction between "straightforward embezzlement" and a "low-life thief who'd steal a man's song." His protestations were not of innocence but of honesty. He never claimed to be innocent. His bizarre reasoning was that he was honest about being dishonest. "I'm a thief," Eugene would say, "but at least I'm honest about it."

The really sobering thought, of course, is to consider the country music singer. How did he justify the theft to himself? *I'm no thief!* he surely tells himself. *I really have no idea where the original idea for that song came from. At least, I never embezzled anything!*

Honesty is the virtue of wealth and words. Honesty in communication is telling the truth. ("Thou shalt not bear false witness.") Honesty in possessions is right action with regard to things. ("Thou shalt not steal.")

That is simple enough. The problem is that we are now facing a generation that morally does not know its left hand

93

from its right. The honest of the earth marveled when President Clinton claimed not to know what "is" means. The simple biblical injunction of the Law of Moses is quaint if not utterly insensible to postmoderns.

HONESTY AND POSSESSIONS

Hardly anyone argues philosophically for theft. Even the thief objects when another thief steals his song. The problem, however, is to see honesty's subtle application to our lives. Many postmodern Americans see theft as armed robbery. Anything short of that, they reason, is actually something else. Casual theft is a major financial and moral problem for America. The teenager who shoplifts, the thrill theft, the unpaid debt—these are the everyday thefts of America. If an individual unnecessarily and deliberately files bankruptcy for the express purpose of avoiding the payment of debt, he is a thief. He has stolen money. It is a dishonest ploy to delay repaying a debt until the creditor, in frustration, simply writes it off. If a housewife arrives at her car and realizes there is one article in her shopping bag that was not actually rung up, and she does not return to pay for it, she is a thief.

Faceless theft has become a justifiable crime. No one excuses robbing an old lady of her social security check, but to steal from an institution has become virtually heroic. It is different to steal from a company or a corporation, many people think.

In Warren Beatty's movie about Clyde Barrow, there is a fascinating bank robbery scene in which a customer stands at the counter with his hands up as Bonnie and Clyde rob the teller. Clyde indicates a stack of loose cash lying on the counter and, turning his gun on the man, asks, "Whose money is this on the counter?"

"It's my money," the man answers. "I haven't made my deposit yet."

"Pick it up," Clyde responds, "and put it in your pocket. I

don't rob individuals. I only rob banks."

His was a specious logic. Yet, tragically, Clyde may have spoken for untold thousands of Americans who find it perfectly acceptable to defraud an insurance company. *After all*, we say to ourselves, *insurance is a racket itself.*

Faceless theft starts with the wrong question. The question is not who or what owns a thing. The greater issue is who does not. Respect for private ownership transcends my ability to identify the owner. The fact that it is not mine is the bottom line. It is irrelevant that I do not know the rightful owner.

Prevailing "wisdom" claims that what I do *not* know is crucial to honesty. If I do not know whose it is, it may as well be mine. We must rearrange our thinking. Honesty must be based on what I do know. I may not know whose it is, but I certainly know whose it is not. Knowing it is not mine is the true ground of honesty. The point is not really that I have no right to what is yours. The point is, I have no right to that which is not mine.

HONEST GAIN

Honest financial advancement is an honorable goal. The selling of worthy goods or services for a fair price is pleasing in God's sight. There is nothing wrong with making a profit and gaining wealth. God wants His people to prosper.

However, the selling of goods for more than they are worth, even though the traffic will bear it, is dishonest. Willfully hiding pertinent information from another in order to get the better of him in a business deal is not shrewd business; it is thievery.

Boynton's Mercedes turned off the main road.
The gravel crunched under its wheels like tiny
bones in the massive jaws of a great wolf. It was a

good, powerful, masculine sound, and he liked it.

A bunny darted across the lane, and he could not resist the impulse to swerve the huge car. He did not hit the cottontail. He did not mean to, but its frightened, erratic journey into the under- growth made him chuckle. "That's one little rabbit with a harrowing tale of near death to share when it gets home."

As he drove, he enjoyed the idyllic scene spread out before him. The leaves on the massive oaks were in full fall plumage. The old gray fence posts and rusted barbed wire traced antique designs across the brown, overgrown fields. In fact, it was hard to believe he was only an hour and a half from downtown. Right here on this lonely gravel road he felt years away from the madding crosstown connector and his own high-rise office building.

Only a few years before, these fields would have been full of cattle. Old lady Watson was not really farming any of this anymore. She had no family to help, and she lived all alone out here.

Why, he was doing her a favor. With the money from this sale, she would be able to live comfort- ably until she died. Getting away from this farm was what she needed. She was lucky he came along. Anyone else might have really robbed her.

His cell phone rang just as the roof and twin chimneys of the Watson farmhouse nudged into view. As he answered, he noted the sagging roof line jutting above the soft, grassy-brown horizon.

"Hello," he answered.

"Hey, Boynton, it's Carl," the smooth voice of his partner responded. "Are you nearly there?"

"Yes," Boynton answered. "I can see the house

from here. Your timing is perfect. What have you got for me? Is our information correct?"

"I checked with Commissioner Threllkell. It looks like the new loop is going right through the old Watson place. Have you got the check and the contract? Is she going to sign?"

"Calm down," Boynton reassured him. "It's in the bag. Are you sure your information is good?"

"I told you," Carl purred. "I talked to Threllkell himself. Of course, he wouldn't officially confirm the route."

"Of course." They both chuckled amiably at the Threllkell joke. Threllkell was a fool, and they both knew it. Two weeks in the Bahamas every year assured Threllkell's unofficial dependability. "See you at the office in a few hours. Gotta go."

"Listen, Boynton, do you think the old lady has heard about the new loop yet?" Carl asked. The directness of the question irritated Boynton. Carl's lack of tact was a constant bother to Boynton.

"Don't be silly," he barked and hung up.

Boynton eased the metallic blue Mercedes to a halt in front of the picturesque old house with its wide-sweeping veranda. *It would be a real shame to knock this thing over*, he thought. A real shame. He stepped out of the Mercedes, stretched his arms over his head and circled the car.

HONEST GAIN HONESTLY GOT

There is a line between shrewd business and dishonesty. However, it is not nearly as fine as we are led to believe. We would do far better to bend over backward for honesty. It is better to miss out on the deal than to make it by the slightest deception. It is better to make a minor profit with honesty than a major one without it.

Of course, honesty in selling is no less important than honesty in buying. Selling something for more than it is worth is dishonest, not clever. The used car lot that sells an automobile knowing that the transmission is on its last leg is operated by a band of thieves. The fact that they do not use guns is irrelevant; they are still brigands.

Gambling has become a controversial issue in the modern church. This controversy became even more public when a high-profile conservative figure confessed to a serious gambling habit. This is a remarkable turn of events. Historically much of the church has emphatically opposed gambling, but there is no specific Bible verse that says, "Thou shalt not gamble." The counsel of God taken as a whole clearly teaches that I have no right to another's goods without offering something of value in return. Gambling not only endangers the resources of God entrusted into my hands, but also I exploit the passion and lust for chance in the life of another in order to take his goods with nothing in return. When a state or a nation begins to operate gambling games, it breeds characterlessness and immorality into the lives of its citizenry.

The great need in America now is for moral leadership. The end *never* justifies the means. Do not be fooled by how many textbooks a state lottery will buy. Consider the single mother in the ghetto who will bet her children's lunch money on a three-digit number.

Likewise, the exaggerated advertisement and the padded expense account have almost become fixtures of American business. Deliberately shaved tax forms are submitted without hesitation, not by Mafia chieftains but by middle-class churchgoers. Employees chronically arrive late and leave early, never even considering their theft of time and salary. Employee theft of tools and goods now reaches into the billions annually.

Possessions are significant because they come from God. They are entrusted into our stewardship. How we handle possessions, our own and those of others, is important. It is important because it is important to God.

HONESTY IN COMMUNICATION

Honesty is correct relationship with the highest level of reality. God Himself is ultimate reality. Truth is sacred because departure from truth is departure from God. The issue of truth is crucial to what we believe to be true about God and life.

Satan is a liar and the father of lies. Those who operate in right relationship to ultimate truth live in right relationship to who God is. They reflect the character of their Father. Those who deal in deception reveal who their true father is. Satan is the father of and the center of all deception in the earth.

TRUE TRUTH AND FALSE TRUTH

There may be things that are true, but they are not the truth. When Abraham and Sarah were in Egypt, Abraham knew the Egyptians would see that Sarah was beautiful and might well desire to have her. Abraham also knew that he was defenseless. If they wanted his wife, they might kill him to take her. He said, "She is my sister," which was true. Sarah was his half-sister. They shared the same father by different mothers. She was technically his sister. The higher reality, of course, was that she was his wife. What Abraham told the Egyptians was true, but it was not the truth.

True statements can even be woven together to form an untruth. The classic example is the first mate who wrote in the log book, "Captain was sober today." The captain may have been sober every day, but the implication was that the captain's sobriety was a happy and rare occurrence. The very way the mate included that statement, a true statement, created an untruth. A true statement can be made an untruth, a destructive untruth that can wreak havoc in any organization.

The first mate, in deception, manipulation and innuendo, brings disharmony into the ship. The second mate sees the spurious entry and asks, "Does the captain have a problem with alcohol?" The first mate says nothing but shrugs his shoulders and rolls his eyes. He has silently lied yet again. Now the first mate goes to the captain and says, "Captain, you just might like to know that the second mate asked me today if you have a chronic problem with alcohol." Again, it was a true statement. Yet it became a sordid, manipulative lie by painting an untrue picture.

In this way the difference is clear between a true statement and the truth. Now a distinction must be made between an untruth and an inaccuracy. A lie has a great deal to do with motive. A father says to his child, "Tomorrow we'll go to the park."

In the night, however, a great earthquake bursts the nation open from sea to sea, and the city park slides into oblivion. The six-year-old who does not know or care about the earthquake joyfully announces, "We're going to the park today."

The father explains, "No, the park is no more. It's gone."

The child pouts, "You lied!" Did the father lie? He certainly did not. Was he inaccurate? He was.

Maturity understands the delicate balance between an inaccuracy, or even a jest and a lie. On the one hand the issue is guile and motive. The problem on the other hand is cold-blooded literalism.

I was visiting in the parsonage of a fellow pastor. He had a cute little four-year-old son. At one point I tweaked the lad's nose, pushing the end of my thumb through my fingers. "I've got your nose!" I announced triumphantly.

The little boy pleaded jokingly, "No, give me back my nose! Give me back my nose!"

Then in a minute I'd grab it again. "Got your nose, got your nose."

After a few minutes his preacher father said, in front of the child, "I'd thank you not to do that again. I make it a practice not to lie to my children, and you're not helping me teach that."

I had, in fact, told the child an untruth. I did not get the boy's nose. I state that now in print. I would have *liked* to have gotten his father's nose. That kind of smug literalism draws a tiny little circle of truth and rejects all the joy of fantasy and creative humor.

Every parent must make the determination about how to relate to truth and fantasy. My wife and I never indulged in the Santa Claus myth with our children. We told our children from the beginning that Santa is strictly a cultural legend. There is, of course, no such thing as Santa Claus, but many fine parents do teach their children to believe in him. We were straightforward with our own children. I felt this determination served our own goals best, but I am not attempting to heap condemnation on anyone. Our own reasons were twofold. One was that we felt it was too closely related to the issue of theology. I did not want to have to explain to a wide-eyed eight-year-old that, yes, I know I told you there was a Santa Claus, but Jesus is actually real.

The second reason was more self-serving. I did not encourage the Santa Claus myth because, I reasoned, why should I shell out all that money every year and let a fat guy in a red suit get all the credit?

Literalism will make our lives joyless and uncreative. Cordell Hull, the secretary of state under Franklin D. Roosevelt, was a notorious literalist. Riding a train across the Midwest, the secretary and some others observed a flock of sheep in a field. Someone said, "I see all these sheep have already been sheared." Cordell Hull protested, "No, I don't think we can safely state that. All we can be sure of is that those sheep have been sheared on the side facing the train."

Having admitted that such literal-minded priggishness is indeed galling, it is equally certain that it is not the greater issue. There are two kinds of dishonest communication. The first is simulation; the second is dissimulation. *Simulation* is to seem to be what we are not. *Dissimulation* is to seem not to be what we are.

SIMULATION

Simulation includes all deceptive practices of image alteration, many of which are deeply ingrained in postmodern society. The craft of simulation includes such tools as exaggeration, pretense and hypocrisy. The image-conscious society in which we live hates truth and loves appearance.

An unspoken pact of mutual deception rules the land like a cruel monarch. You pretend to believe my image, and I will pretend to accept yours. We both know the other is spinning out simulation like a spider's web. We both know it is not reality, and we both know the other knows it. Yet we agree to the silent mutual deception because it suits us both.

Religion, no less than politics or business, plays this simulation game. Sometimes it is no more than mere exaggeration to appear more spiritual or caring or successful than we really are. Sometimes it is the crass, Hollywood manipulation of television audiences and Sunday congregations for evil purposes.

One Sunday afternoon as I was visiting another parsonage, we all enjoyed a lovely dinner and settled in to watch a football game. At halftime the pastor got up and left the room for ten minutes or so. Later at the evening service, before I was to preach, the pastor told the congregation, "I just want to tell you that I made a pastoral call this afternoon. I spent some time with Sister Wilson. She's much better."

I was frankly amazed to hear this report. After the service I said to the pastor, "You know, we've been friends for a long time, and I'm not trying to call your hand. I just want to understand. You said you went to the hospital, but we watched football all afternoon. I don't think there's anything wrong with two preachers watching football, but you said you went to the hospital."

He laughed and said, "No, I didn't. I never said I actually went to the hospital. You weren't listening. Remember when I went out at halftime? I spent ten minutes on the phone with that lady."

"Yes," I replied, "but you gave your people the impression that you went to the hospital."

"What does it hurt if they think their pastor made a visit on Sunday afternoon instead of watching a ball game?" he asked.

The story of Ananias and Sapphira is evidence of God's seriousness about religious simulation (Acts 5:1–11). They were not slain for withholding money. They died for claiming more generosity and gracious faith than they had. Their sobering story is about honesty in matters spiritual.

It was shocking and repulsive to read about the bogus evangelist who claimed to operate in the word of knowledge while actually receiving radio transmissions from a hidden sound booth. What a reproach! What a horrifying scandal! The man will certainly answer to God, but the American church is not blameless. The American church has actually created an atmosphere that is conducive to such simulation. We are sending ministries mixed signals. We financially support ministries that are experts in simulation, and then hate them when they are exposed. We embrace the hyperspiritual, flamboyant image-makers and their puppet preachers. We demand that they *not* tell us the truth, but we despise their public nakedness.

DISSIMULATION

Dissimulation is appearing *not* to be what we really are. This is perhaps the more common crisis of faith for the average Western believer.

The soft conversation and rippling good humor among those lounging in the courtyard belied the tragedy being played out inside. It made it easier for the burly fisherman to rest unnoticed against the wall of the high priest's house. It was crazy for him to be here. If they had arrested Jesus Himself, His followers would be in even greater danger.

He just couldn't stay away. Confused, disoriented and nearly distraught, he had followed the miserable little band of temple guards from Olivet to the Antonia fortress and on to this foreboding place. He should leave. What could he do to help? Yet something rooted him to the ground.

With the evening closing in on Peter like a clammy hand, he shivered and drew his robe tighter. Peter stared at the flickering torch light from within Caiaphas' mansion. The random outbursts and shouting from inside filled him with fear and dread. The night watchman, several cronies and a couple of bored soldiers stood near a bed of glowing embers. The fire drew Peter like a magnet. Soon his massive hands were warming over the radiant coals.

"Here's one of them," a girl's voice interrupted his mournful thoughts. "That big guy is a follower of Jesus."

Across the fire from him a slender adolescent pointed her delicate finger right between his eyes. His grief and concern for his Master drained quickly away, and in its place came a flood of fear. Peter had never felt so naked. Was this the way he would end? Denounced in a shadowy courtyard by a mere servant girl?

The soldiers around him stirred. Their interest mildly awakened, they turned their eyes on the craggy figure who shared their fire. Peter sensed instantly that this could get very dangerous in moments. These wolves awakened could be lethal.

Peter began to curse and swear. "I tell you, I don't know this Jesus. I don't know the man!"

Now, no matter how close to the fire he stood, Peter could not seem to get warm. Surely this courtyard was the coldest place in Israel on this evil night. (See Matthew 26:69–75.)

Most Christians will never be tempted to deny Christ before a firing squad. Few, relatively speaking, will be tortured to denounce His name. Far more often it is by silence or a head nod or a knowing wink that the modern believer denies his allegiance to Christ. "I do not know Him" is the subtle dissimulation of the collaborator. The hypocrite pretends to be what he is not. The compromised, lacking the courage of their convictions, deny who they are.

Let your "yea be yea and your nay be nay," the Bible says. (See Matthew 5:37.) That may very well mean saying *yes* to Jesus when it is costly and *no* to the world when it is unpopular. The temptation will seldom be to outright denial, but rather to subtle compromises. Soft public dissimulation is the velvet-lined coffin of bold and dynamic faith.

THE INSTINCT FOR DISHONESTY

The motivation for dishonesty is the animal instinct for self-preservation. The flesh says, "If I want it, I'll steal it. If I am not, I'll pretend to be. If I am, I'll pretend not to be. If I want to sell it, I will not tell everything." What can possibly shatter the spell of so inborn an instinct?

Proverbs 22:4 says, "By humility and the fear of the Lord are riches, and honour, and life." Babies are not born with the fear of God. They are born with sin and an instinct for survival. Parents, governments, schools and institutions are to instill the fear of God. If they fail in that duty, how will character ever be engraved upon young lives? In every human heart there is the thumbprint of the Creator. It is a homesickness for the image of God. Once awakened, this longing for a character and godliness is a fierce power, and there is great joy in moving from glory to glory.

The closer a man lives to reality and truth, the more fully this inner longing is awakened. "Ye shall know the truth, and the truth shall make you free" (John 8:32) is not mere church rhetoric. It is the mystery key to full humanity in the image of God.

Cynical Pilate, staring quizzically into the face of the Lamb of God, asked his infamous question: "What is truth?"

Now listen to the answer of God.

> I am the way, the truth, and the life.
>
> —JOHN 14:6

CHAPTER 8

MEEKNESS: CHARACTER AND POWER

Its young men gone to death or in prisoner of war camps far in the North, its heartland in ashes and its agriculture and industry destroyed, the South, in 1865, was shattered. Postwar poverty and a deep sense of shame and defeat gripped the states of the former confederacy with economic and psycho-social depression.

The victorious North had not escaped the horrible civil conflict without its own wounds. The rolls of the dead and wounded filled whole pages of the northern newspapers. The federal army had won a Pyrrhic victory at best. Then, as reports of the atrocities in camps such as Andersonville became more public, the screams for revenge grew louder and more demanding. Many in power wanted the defeated South crushed and humiliated. The army and the congress wanted the conquered rebel states occupied, gutted and forever stripped of full participation in the republic.

Lincoln, as war-weary as any, with as great a reason for vengeance as they, would have none of it. Whatever demeaning and vindictive excesses were perpetrated during "reconstruction," none were Lincoln's fault. The South had rebelled, had cost the lives of thousands and had devastated a generation for the sake of an unjust and immoral cause.

Lincoln, with the power to punish them bitterly or even to return slavery for slavery, longed instead to return the wayward safely to the fold.

Abraham Lincoln, sixteenth president of the United States, had the South at his feet after Appomattox. His closest advisors, even his own cabinet, urged him to step on the naked throat of the defeated Confederacy and press down. Only his meekness, his refusal to use his power in unrestrained vengeance, saved the South and the nation from a postwar nightmare even worse than it was.

Lincoln, long known for his honesty, proved the depth of his great and noble character with meekness. In his second inaugural address, with the rebellious states of the confederacy on their knees and the union clamoring for revenge, Lincoln boldly called on Americans for healing love:

> With malice toward none, with charity for all, with firmness in the right as God gives us to see the right, let us strive on to finish the work we are in, to bind up the nation's wounds, to care for him who shall have borne the battle and for his widow and his orphan, to do all which may achieve and cherish a just and lasting peace among ourselves and with all nations.[1]

God bless thee; and put meekness in thy mind,
love, charity, obedience and true duty!
—WILLIAM SHAKESPEARE

T HE GREATNESS OF THE POWERFUL is made manifest in restraint. Meekness is the virtue of the victor, not the vanquished. Meekness is the manliest virtue. Misunderstood by many, meekness is often thought to be only for the weak-sister types. Nothing could be further from the truth. Meekness is the supreme virtue of leadership without which power becomes tyranny. Meekness is power under control. Christianity itself is a paradox that turns topside down the world's comprehension of what it means to live triumphantly. In that sense meekness is Christianity's epitomal virtue.

Now in all virtues there is what might be called the conviction of the virtue. That is what we believe to be true about it. Then there is its theater of operation. That is, some circumstance is necessary to put the virtue in action. Fear, for example, must be present or courage cannot be called into action. Just so, the ascent to power is the universe of meekness.

A big boy hits a small boy. The small boy endures it quietly because he has no other option. Inwardly, however, he seethes with lust for revenge. Because he is subdued in the face of violence, we may mislabel him as meek. Yet he is actually consumed with murderous rage. He forgoes vengeance, but he is not meek. He is simply resigned. If, however, the small boy hits the larger fellow, it is the offended party who has the power. He can break the smaller boy in half, yet he bears it quietly. That's meekness.

There are two words that taken together paint a completely wrong picture of meekness. Those two words are *meek* and *little*. We often say, "He is a meek little fellow." Immediately a sort of Casper Milquetoast image is conjured up. We envision this man as an impotent, powerless bloke. In reality, however, we would be better to say, "What a big, strong, powerful, rugged meek fellow." When we identify meekness with being effete, we pervert the virtue.

Meekness is not even possible until power is at risk. We can learn meekness in the company of lions. The mother lion lies quietly with her cubs playing about her. In their weakness they nip each other with all their strength. Watching them, we may think they are just playing. They are not playing. They are fighting. They are learning to be full-grown lions. They simply do not have the power to hurt each other. They are biting with all their might, but their little jaws are like the pincers of crabs. They nip and pinch and irritate, but they cannot possibly inflict serious wounds.

Now behold the great lioness with strength in her jaws sufficient to snap the hind legs of a full-grown impala. She reaches down and picks up the cubs in her fearsome mouth. She has the power to snuff out their lives, yet the babies lie quietly and safely between her ominous jaws. She, not the cubs, is meek.

Meekness is rarely provoked. It is easily pacified. It is controlled, patient and easily entreated. It is willing to forgive when forgiveness will earn no reward. Meekness is love in the driver's seat.

When a culture distorts meekness to become weakness, its leaders grow increasingly ruthless. "Might makes right" becomes the motto of such a culture, and the weak are plowed under. Indeed, the weak in any society depend for protection, not on the mighty, but on the meek. When meekness disappears, the most defenseless elements of the society are at risk.

Take, for example, the relationship between mother and

child. The infant, born or unborn, is subject to its mother's power. Life and death are in her hands. The argument for abortion in the name of a woman's right to choose could only arise in a cultural atmosphere where meekness is devalued. Postmodern Western society sees no virtue in meekness, and mothers grow more ruthless in their power.

THE MEEKNESS OF JESUS CHRIST

Everything was spoken into existence, and nothing that we see was made without the Lord Jesus. Unto Him all things will return. It is appropriate for Him to consider Himself as having full rights in the Godhead. He is the second person of the triune God! Yet, having full authority in the Godhead, He laid all that aside and clothed Himself in mere mortality. Being found in the form of a man, He took upon Himself the likeness of a servant. (See Philippians 2:6–7.) (The word that is translated "servant" in the King James Version might even better be rendered "slave.")

Therefore, Paul admonishes us to own up to Christ's way of thinking. We are called to embrace His whole approach to living. Christ Jesus laid aside His rights as God to become not only a man but a slave of men. Born in an occupied country under the authority of foreign soldiers, He was crucified by men whom He had created. God, willing to lay aside His authority over the earth and become man, is meekness perfected.

THE BLESSINGS OF THE MEEK

There are great promises for the meek. Miss the virtue and miss the blessings.

Christlikeness

Matthew 11:29 is an illuminating passage of Scripture:

> Take my yoke upon you, and learn of me; for I am meek and lowly in heart: and ye shall find rest unto your souls.

We must settle ourselves into the double yoke with Jesus on one side and us on the other. The ox yoke thus securely around our necks, we learn His meekness. When He turns left, we turn left. When He turns right, we turn right. We learn to walk at His pace, to move when He moves and to stand still when He stops. When He pauses, we wait patiently. We fit ourselves to Him. We learn of Him; therefore, we learn about Him. The longer we walk with Him, the more we walk like Him. The longer we talk with Him, the more we talk like Him. Like two old married people, we grow to look more alike.

Happiness

Meekness brings happiness in this life. It makes a man fit to live with because he is not easily threatened by the loss of his power. Not constantly striving to gain dominance, the meek reject tactics of manipulation and intimidation.

Meekness likewise makes a man fit to do business with. The meek will not do business out of competitive neurosis. Not needing to "get the upper hand" in every deal, the meek are to be trusted. Furthermore, because they are honest, the meek tend to prosper.

The meek will be happy in this life not only because they are fit to be with and fit to deal with, but also because they are able to be alone. A man who cannot stand to be alone with himself is a miserable person. A meek man, satisfied with the yoke of Jesus, is perfectly happy to be alone because he is, in fact, not alone. He who guides his footsteps also communes with him in the secret place.

Inheritance

The meek shall inherit the earth. In Lerner and Loewe's musical comedy *Camelot*, the frustrated knights sarcastically proclaim, "It's not the earth the meek inherit; it's the dirt."[2] They were wrong. To *inherit* means to come into authority, to gain dominion over. Matthew 5 may refer to the earth that

God used to form our own "earthen vessels" (2 Cor. 4:7). Self-possession, dominion over appetites and passions, is the inheritance of the meek. The meek inherit—they have dominion over their own earthen vessels.

There is also a future tense application to the promise. There *is* a new earth coming, an earth so beautiful and so perfect that it is not to be inherited by the grasping power-mongers of this age. This flawless new earth will be reserved only for the meek.

It is not the dirt the meek inherit. It *is* the earth. After this earth is burned away along with its corrupt military, political and economic power systems, the meek shall live and reign with Him eternally.

I was in West Africa some years ago at the Wycliffe Summer Institute of Linguistics. While there, I met an old German missionary. She was in her seventies, had river blindness and was on her way home to die. In the place where we stayed, her room was down the hall from mine. One day I watched her inch her way down the hallway tracing her hand along the wall.

A Ghanaian who was with me said, "Do you know that old lady has single-handedly translated the entire New Testament into two languages? She has two complete New Testaments to her credit. She's one of the greatest translators Wycliffe has ever had. Now she's contracted river blindness and is going back to Germany to die, but she has no family left. She's just going there to die."

Later, on my own flight home I saw in the London *Times* a picture of Colonel Muammar Qaddafi as he rode in his car down the streets of Tripoli. The crowds in the photo, their rifles in the air, were cheering wildly. Their guns blazed as their warrior chief rode down the middle of the street. There was something in me that flared up. I resented the thought of an absolute criminal, a gangster, being celebrated as a hero by multiplied hundreds of thousands, while that precious old saint died in obscurity.

Then the Holy Spirit came and comforted me. "When the rifles of Libya are silent and Qaddafi is answering for his life, she will receive an inheritance incorruptible and undefiled that fadeth not away."

Guidance

According to Psalm 25:9, God will guide the meek into what is right and teach them His way. Because of that, the meek live in peace instead of in the world's confusion and turmoil. The meek, submitted to the yoke of God, resting in His will, live without all the striving, agonizing, gut-wrenching fear that grips the minds of the masses.

JUDGMENT FOR MEEKNESS

God Himself, says Psalm 76:9, will judge and save all the meek of the earth. The meek can rest themselves in the face of injustices, because ultimately God will set it right. I find that when we are the most outraged over injustice, we are most likely to lose touch with meekness. Meekness takes the patient, long-run view of God's justice. The Book of Revelation says that the blood of the martyrs cries out from underneath the altar. "How long, O God? How long, O God, until You arise and judge the earth?" (See Revelation 6:10.)

There is something in us that longs to see the judgment of God visited on those that make terrorists and tyrants out to be heroes. There is, however, a balance. We dare not turn a blind eye to injustices and become complacent, but justice and vengeance are not the same. God has ordained that on this earth civil government bears the sword for the purpose of rendering justice (Rom. 13:1–4). God can use the armies of the earth to punish the wicked, but the spirit of meekness will leave judgment to God. Vengeance and wrath are not emotions that humans are capable of handling. The reason God says, "Vengeance is Mine," is not because vengeance is wrong. Vengeance is right. It must come, but it must never be in the wrong hands. We are insufficient to the task.

Vengeance in our hands will destroy us. We are not God, and vengeance is a godly thing.

MEEKNESS IN LEADERSHIP

Meekness in every level of society is important, but it is absolutely essential in leadership. The distortion or loss of meekness in political, military, economic and religious leadership will thoroughly pervert any culture.

Ascending to the throne at his father's death, young Rehoboam sought counsel. To follow Solomon's fame and glory was no easy task for the young king. He needed wisdom.

> And king Rehoboam consulted with the old men, that stood before Solomon his father while he yet lived, and said, How do ye advise that I may answer this people? And they spake unto him, saying, If thou wilt be a servant unto this people this day, and wilt serve them, and answer them, and speak good words to them, then they will be thy servants for ever.
> —1 KINGS 12:6–7

The graybeards—the elders who understood, who knew that character and servanthood were necessary in the leader of a nation—advised that he be meek. The young men, outraged at such an idea, gave very different counsel.

> And he said unto them, What counsel give ye that we may answer this people, who have spoken to me, saying, Make the yoke which thy father did put upon us lighter? And the young men that were grown up with him spake unto him, saying, Thus shalt thou speak unto this people that spake unto thee, saying, Thy father made our yoke heavy, but make thou it lighter unto us; thus shalt thou say unto them, My little finger shall be thicker than my father's loins.
> —1 KINGS 12:9–10

Their blatant appeal to Rehoboam's insecurity won out.

The obscene comparison between Rehoboam and his father, Solomon, did not miss the mark either. It may have been sophomoric and irrational, but it touched the raw nerves of Rehoboam's self-doubts.

The nation shuddered at the new king's first speech. "Solomon, my father, chastised you with whips, I will chastise you with scorpions." (See 1 Kings 12:11.) Rehoboam made it clear that he was no man's servant.

The CEO who wants to lead in the style of Jesus takes upon himself the mantle of meekness. He never asks himself how his employees can further his career, but seeks instead to help his employees fulfill their potential as human beings and productive members of society.

The meek pastor does not ask how his staff, elders and membership can help fulfill his ambitions. He asks himself, rather, what he can do that will bring *them* into the fullness of the stature of Christ. The politician who is meek does not ask himself what the people can do to carve his niche in history. He seeks some way to bless the least member of his constituency.

There was a city, an ancient and barbaric city, that needed a new king. They called four of their leading citizens and said to each, "We're offering you the opportunity to be king of the city."

The key of the city was placed on a table before each man, one at a time.

The first was a warrior, a brave and courageous warrior whose exploits in battle had won him great fame. They said, "Put both of your hands palm down on the table." The key of the city lay between them.

They said, "If you want to be king badly

enough, you would be willing to lose one of your hands."

A man with an axe stood ominously at each end of the table. "If you want the key, you may grasp it," said the people. "You can only move one of your hands, and the other one will be cut off. If you grasp the key with your right hand, the key is yours, and you will be the king, but you will lose your left."

The warrior wanted to be king more than anything else, so he reasoned within himself, *My right hand is my sword hand; I dare not lose it. My right hand is the source of my strength and power.* Deciding to lose his left hand, he grabbed the key with his right hand.

Those barbaric citizens cruelly chopped off his left hand and cast him out of the city. "Remnant, you are not worthy to be our king!"

The second was a philosopher. Not knowing the fate of the warrior, he struggled with the same question. They said to him, in turn, "Choose one." He reasoned within himself, *I write with my left hand, and the strength of my life is creativity. Therefore I will grasp the key with my left hand and let them chop off my right.* The cruel city amputated the philosopher's right hand and cast him out of the city. "You are not worthy to be our king."

The third man was the richest merchant in the city. He did not know the fate of the other two. All he saw before him was the golden key and all the riches and power that it implied. His greed consumed him and not thinking, he clutched the key with both hands. They cast him handless out of the city.

The fourth was a farmer. With the key between his hands, the question was put to him. He quickly withdrew both hands. The farmer

explained, "My hands are my only means of
service in this harsh world. I will not sacrifice any
of my ability to grow food for my fellow man
merely for the sake of power." Instantly every cit-
izen of the kingdom fell at his feet and crowned
him king. They said, "Only one who despises
power is worthy to have it."

LEADERS WITHOUT MEEKNESS

Leadership without meekness deeply engraved in its character always corrupts itself in one way or another. Leaders
lacking meekness fall into three categories.

Category 1: Distant Emperor

King Ahasuerus was unapproachable, infallible and unable
to make a mistake. In the Book of Esther, anyone approaching
this ancient king without being summoned, including his wife,
would die if the king did not extend his scepter. This king
could kill by simply sitting motionless. The father or husband
without meekness is a glacial mountain, frozen, distant and
silent. Out of fear of rejection, he withdraws into a shell of
protection, and any who approach unbidden may die.

The meek leader lays down the scepter of authority and
makes himself approachable. The meek leader is able to
admit others into his real presence, not sentencing them to
the death of separation and seclusion.

Category 2: Macho Man

This type is threatened by his own inadequacies, fearful that
he is not altogether male. He repeatedly celebrates his own
maleness, constantly seeking to tighten his fragile hold on mas-
culinity, thus reminding himself, "I'm a male. I'm a male. I'm a
male." Ironically enough, there is often a paper-thin mem-
brane separating Macho Man and the effeminate homosexual.

Category 3: Suffering Martyr

This leader, tired and nearly beaten, has paid the price for his family. When his authority is questioned or his will is challenged, he responds by showing how put upon and wounded he is. Not domineering but manipulative, his character has, none the less, lost meekness.

Many actually mistake Suffering Martyr for a man of meekness. In reality he is bankrupt. He has retreated behind a wall of grieved condescension. Suffering Martyr is so right and so far above others that he cannot even attempt to explain his pain and sorrow. His is cowardly and unjust leadership. Furthermore, Suffering Martyr has lost a key element of balanced, mature living and leadership. He has lost his sense of humor.

A sense of humor is not the ability to detect what is funny. A sense of humor is the ability to laugh at oneself. If someone else slips on a banana peel and you laugh, that has little to do with your sense of humor. If *you* slip on a banana peel and laugh, you have a sense of humor. A meek leader will laugh at his own pratfall. Suffering Martyr sees *nothing* funny about his plight. The meek leader receives both criticism and compliments with humor and therefore with balance.

MEEKNESS AND REBELLION

Chafing under the leadership of their brother Moses, Miriam and Aaron began to reason in the flesh and not in the Spirit. Surely Moses did not have a corner on the God market. They were as mature as he. In fact, when Moses had fled to Midian, they had remained in Egypt. They had out-suffered Moses if nothing else. Then there was this matter of the foreign woman. Moses' Gentile wife galled them.

Aaron was a prophet. As for Miriam, was she excluded because she was a woman? God could not be so unjust. *Moses*, not God, was their complaint. They were as good as

Moses, and they wanted their fair share of the power. Finally, in Numbers 12, their inner rebellion burst into the open. Comparing their ministry and spirituality with his, Aaron and Miriam laid at least partial claim on leadership.

> Now the man Moses was very meek, above all the
> men which were upon the face of the earth.
> —NUMBERS 12:3

Because of his meekness, Moses never once struggled to retain power. He left that to God. Moses did not speak for Moses; God spoke for Moses.

> And the LORD spake suddenly unto Moses, and unto
> Aaron, and unto Miriam, Come out ye three unto
> the tabernacle of the congregation. And they three
> came out. And the LORD came down in the pillar of
> the cloud, and stood in the door of the tabernacle,
> and called Aaron and Miriam: and they both came
> forth. And he said, Hear now my words: If there be
> a prophet among you, I the LORD will make myself
> known unto him in a vision, and will speak unto him
> in a dream. My servant Moses is not so, who is
> faithful in all mine house. With him will I speak
> mouth to mouth, even apparently, and not in dark
> speeches; and the similitude of the LORD shall he
> behold: wherefore then were ye not afraid to speak
> against my servant Moses?
>
> And the anger of the LORD was kindled against
> them; and he departed. And the cloud departed from
> off the tabernacle; and, behold, Miriam became lep-
> rous, white as snow: and Aaron looked upon
> Miriam, and, behold, she was leprous.
>
> And Aaron said unto Moses, Alas, my lord, I
> beseech thee, lay not the sin upon us, wherein we
> have done foolishly, and wherein we have sinned.
> Let her not be as one dead, of whom the flesh is half
> consumed when he cometh out of his mother's

> womb. And Moses cried unto the LORD, saying,
> Heal her now, O God, I beseech thee.
> —NUMBERS 12:4–13

The first time Moses spoke in the entire passage was to intercede for Miriam's healing. Moses did not spring to the defense of his own ministry, nor did he struggle to hold on to the reins of authority. He simply said, "God gave me this. If God wants me to have it, it is God's business. If God no longer wants me to have it, that is God's business, too." That is the spirit of meekness.

The Hebrew word for *meekness* has an intriguing alternate translation. It is "disinterested." Read Numbers 12:3 that way.

> Now the man Moses was very [disinterested], above
> all the men which were upon the face of the earth.

Moses said, "I have no vested interest in this matter. This is the Lord's business, and these are God's people. It is God's tabernacle, God's power and God's glory. It is God's nation and God's business. I am personally disinterested. God can do whatever He wants."

Aaron and Miriam, in their murmuring, lusted for authority and power. Moses was quite willing for God to lift the mantle from him and choose another.

To the arrogant, self-centered husband claiming to be "the head of the household," God says, "Learn the meekness of Moses." As the God-appointed leader of a nation, Moses wanted the last baby safely across the Red Sea. He was infinitely concerned that each of his people live in the holiness of God. Concerning who was to be boss, Moses was flatly disinterested.

The pastor who stands in the pulpit constantly crying, "I am the boss. I am the boss," has missed the meaning of pastor as servant. The servant-pastor says to his people, "What I want for you is what God wants for you. My only purpose in being in this ministry is for you to know all that God has for you."

It is in a great part a lack of meekness in leadership that causes strikes that bankrupt industries. The CEO who says to the rank and file, "Make my dreams come true! Work harder. Make me rich," is asking for union trouble. Characterlessness, a lack of meekness in leadership, can bring industry to its knees. The servant-leader, the meek leader has the character to lead successfully.

THE CHARACTER OF THE MEEK LEADER

First, his achievements may be great, but they appear not to be his alone. Second, his transforming influence may touch many, but those thus touched do not learn to depend on him. Third, his subordinates admire his virtues greatly but are free to explore their own strengths without fear of his domination. Fourth, the meek leader is not afraid of the responsibility of leadership, but his authority does not dictate to him who he is. Rather his meekness informs the demonstration of his authority for the good of those whom he serves.

The apostles asked, "Lord, who will be the greatest in Your kingdom?" For an answer Jesus took a basin of water, wrapped a towel around His waist and began to wash their feet. Later when the might of pagan Rome unleashed a holocaust against Christ's followers, that abiding memory of a God-man willing to wash their feet gave them the power to topple an empire without drawing a sword.

CHAPTER 9

REVERENCE:
CHARACTER AND THE SACRED

On Sunday you won't find any chicken or anything else to eat at any of Truett Cathy's one-thousand-plus restaurants. Blasted by critics as legalistic, mocked by detractors for missing out on at least one-seventh of his potential revenue, yet amazingly successful, Cathy's quiet refusal to do business on Sunday remains unaltered by the bemusement of postmodern America.

The annual gross income of Chick-fil-A is estimated to be above one billion dollars. That means that the company is missing out on at least 166 million dollars annually. In fact, the amount lost is probably much more since Sunday, in most restaurants, is usually one of the best days, ironically enough, because of the after-church crowd. None of that will change Cathy's mind. He remains steadfast. Officials at Chick-fil-A are clear: "Admittedly, closing all of our restaurants every Sunday makes us a rarity in this day and age. But it's a little habit that has always served us well, so we're planning to stick with it."

When he launched his first restaurant in 1946, Truett Cathy made the decision to remain closed on Sundays. A loving, generous and gracious man, Cathy never condemns those who do business or eat out on Sundays. His decision is his own, made out of his sense of reverence.

Cathy's was not a cold, legalistic decision but one made out of respect for the things of God. In an age of casual disregard for things sacred, Cathy has earned the respect of even his severest critics. A successful businessman, a generous philanthropist and a lover of humanity, this giant of commerce is also a man of quiet reverence. Money or no money, the parking lot will be empty this Sunday at Truett Cathy's place.

Truett Cathy "wanted to ensure that every Chick-fil-A employee and restaurant operator had an opportunity to worship, spend time with family and friends or just plain rest from the work week. Made sense then, still makes sense now."[1]

A NY MAN'S TRUE CHARACTER IS known not so much by what he learns or earns or owns, but by what he reverences. Likewise, entire civilizations are shaped by what they revere. As worth is assigned to things, persons and institutions, a society carves out its character.

A society that revered murderers above doctors, for example, would surely become increasingly violent. However, when the contrast is as obvious as that between doctors and murderers, the point is hardly subtle. It becomes a bit less apparent when the choice is between doctors who do murder (that is, a "successful" abortionist) and sewer workers who do not do murder.

If virtue is reverenced, virtue increases. If virtueless success or characterless talent is admired above all, character erodes. If impious rock stars are admired above pious clergymen, the national character is stressed to the breaking point. A dangerous step toward collapse is taken when blatant irreverence is touted as a virtue.

Modern American humor is frighteningly irreverent. In the light of the whole counsel of God we must recapture the sober reality that there are some things that are not to be made fun of. What is sacred to God must not be funny to us. Americans tend to say, "This movie was blasphemous and wicked and horrible and murderous and pornographic, but it was so funny," as though that excuses everything.

In an interview, a certain TV performer on a popular comedy show explained the huge success of the program. He said that in part it had been the talent of the people involved. He explained further that their success came from their determination that absolutely nothing was sacred. That "nothing is sacred" may well prove to be the epitaph of the West.

There are some things that are sacred, some things about which we simply should not make jokes. To jest of those things that are high and holy is to intrude dangerously on the things of God.

A massive advertising campaign was used to promote a recent motion picture. Its producers proudly proclaimed the picture as being "wildly irreverent, the 'must-see' picture of the summer." It is discouraging enough when we somehow justify entertainment despite its irreverence, but when a movie's irreverence is its major recommendation, sin has become virtue, and virtue has become sin.

During the war in Iraq, a high school basketball player refused to face the flag during the national anthem. Her personal politics or stance on the war notwithstanding, she refused to honor her own national emblem. The very liberties that guaranteed her the right to do what she did were won at the cost of blood shed to keep that banner waving. It was not her politics that were so reprehensible. It was her irreverence.

What is revered and how such reverence is demonstrated is crucial to a society's character. In other words, appropriate objects of reverence must be chosen and assigned their proper values. Then, appropriate means of demonstrating that reverence, ceremonial and otherwise, must be found.

REVERENCE AND RESPECT

Lecturing in African classrooms, I discovered that my students stood beside their desks when their teachers enter the room. I have often wondered if such respect for teachers can ever again be taught in American classrooms.

Many years ago I taught for a while in Washington, DC. That job afforded me the unhappy experience of escorting a group of junior high students to the National Gallery of Art. I found the experience not unlike attending a debutante ball with the Hell's Angels. The reason it was so exasperating was not merely their bad behavior but the painful sense of casting pearls before swine. I kept asking, "Don't you understand? This is a Renoir."

They would answer, "Hey, Renoir ain't nothing in my book. Do they have a sports section?"

They cared nothing for Gauguin or Van Gogh. Michelangelo was a nobody. They wanted action photos of basketball stars. The beauty or history of various works was totally wasted on them. Worse was their belligerent refusal to learn, to be taught or shown a greatness and beauty that was new to them. What irritated me most was not that we had different tastes. It was their absolute determination not to be changed or illumined or, most of all, impressed.

This is not to advocate highbrow artistic tastes as the ultimate. It is rather to say that there is a danger in the loss of humility necessary to see that a thing is simply wonderful, that it is worthy of my taking notice. The risk of being stuffy and overly formal is real. The risk on the other side of losing respect, dignity and reverence altogether is infinitely greater. Reverence is directly related to humility. There is nothing more obnoxious than arrogant brats who are bored with life.

REVERENCE AND AWE

Our society has cultivated a deliberate boredom, a jaded resistance to being amazed, to wonder at anything. Many

Americans spend their lives bored with everything and are themselves, therefore, monumentally boring. There are certain things that simply demand a response. It is arrogant and self-centered to stand for the first time at the foot of Mount Fuji and say, "Ho hum, it's about what I thought." How infinitely more interesting life is with a person who is unafraid to say, "I never dreamed it would be so beautiful!"

I was with some businessmen at a great luxury hotel where I was to speak. The hotel was a wonderment. In the lobby was the largest indoor atrium I have ever seen, a virtual tropical rainforest. Above it all the guests strolled on elevated walkways affording beautiful vistas in every direction. It was fabulous!

One evening as I walked with several men from the convention, I was extolling its virtues. After a few moments of my *oohs* and *ahs*, one of my embarrassed friends said, "You know, Dr. Rutland, people are going to think you've never seen anything like this before."

I said, "I haven't! I am impressed with this hotel. Aren't you?"

They sheepishly, and only after furtive glances about, admitted they were.

There is something arrogant about a person who refuses to be impressed with anything. We must teach the young a sense of wonder. There are certain things in the presence of which I simply ought to be astonished.

The parents of a bored eleven-year-old took him to the Grand Canyon. He seemed unable to be impressed with anything. Standing at a certain overlook, the boy finally expressed awe at one of the guide's statistics.

"This is a half-mile straight down? Wow!" the boy exclaimed.

"Yes," answered the guide patiently.

"You're sure?" the boy pressed him.

"Yes. That is a half-mile straight drop," the ranger assured him.

"Wow!" the boy kept saying. "Wow!"

That night when their son was sound asleep, the happy parents crept into his room to read his diary entry for the day. They were happy that at last the boy had been impressed with *something*. The lad's diary entry read: "Wow! Today I could spit a half mile."

In the classical, antiquated English use, *reverence* is a verb, meaning to bow before, to make obeisance. It is frequently used in that sense in the Old Testament. To reverence is to show respect, to accord some exalted or sacred status. That respect may be at a level that, depending on culture, may require a bow or a special signal such as a military salute. To reverence the flag, one places hand on heart. To show proper respect may mean to stand silently. Still again, reverence may simply be a matter of the heart and require no outward demonstration.

Reverencing things outside myself tears my eyes off my own importance. When I cultivate the virtue of reverence, of right estimation, I cut away at my natural tendency to make myself the center of all things. The perspective that reverence returns to my life is not only spiritually important, but also it is crucial to emotional well-being.

A certain woman in a state of depression went to a psychiatrist. At the end of the six weeks of $150-an-hour sessions, the doctor said, "I'm going to write a prescription now that will cure you."

He wrote this on the prescription pad: "Go to Niagara Falls. Check into a motel. Leave your suitcase. Go to the falls. Stand on the bottom observation platform and stare up at Niagara Falls for five hours. Repeat this every day for a week, and you'll be cured."

"You quack!" she howled. "I pay you almost a thousand dollars for six sessions, and you tell me to go stare at a waterfall. What are you thinking of?"

"Lady," he explained, "I have met with you for six weeks

at $150 an hour. I told you to talk to me about anything you wanted. All you talk about is yourself; *your* dreams, *your* nightmares, *your* worries, *your* fears and *your* past. The only thing you need to get well is to see something bigger than you are."

A contributing factor to the increasing madness of Western culture is the decline of reverence. The loss of character in the West, particularly the loss of reverence, is a subtle madness. Man at the center of his own life, with all his neuroses and fears, unable to get his eyes off himself, is destined for emotional and spiritual collapse. Alone, man cannot stand the weight of himself.

ADMIRATION AND WORTHSHIP

The question, of course, is what to reverence. Statesmanship is the mastery of statecraft. Churchmanship is the proper stewarding of resources in the activities of the church. Likewise, to assign worth properly is worthship. From just this combination of words we get the single word "worship." Character is weakened when worship is forsaken.

As individuals and societies assign worth, order priorities and choose values, character is formed. "Worthship" ranges then from its lowest expression, mere respect, all the way to its highest, what I worship as God.

Admiration of particular individuals is one aspect of reverence. It is not wrong to admire certain qualities, abilities or achievements of individuals. We must, however, be vigilant against admiring wicked men.

Proverbs 17:15 says, "He that justifieth the wicked, and he that condemneth the just, even they both are abomination to the LORD."

He that esteems righteousness too lowly and he that esteems unrighteousness too highly are an abomination to God. To idolize immoral actors, drug-addicted rock stars and characterless ball players is to revere the unrighteous.

We should show respect and admiration for achievements made in any field of endeavor, yet never forget that character remains infinitely more important.

Years ago a baseball player achieved a great statistical landmark in his career. My son, very young at the time, read the newspaper accounts with fevered excitement. "Oh, Daddy, look at what this guy has done! I would love to be like him."

I took Travis up on my lap and explained my convictions to him. "Travis, I understand what you're saying. There's never been a little boy who didn't want his name on the front page of the sports section. I understand that. But if you grow up to be like that man, Daddy couldn't stand it. I simply could not stand it. That man has been immoral with women. He's a lying, conniving, hard-drinking, hard-swearing, corrupt human being. He can swing a baseball bat, but he is a failure as a man. His life is out of control. The Bible says that a man whose life is out of control is like a city with the walls broken down.

"Travis, it's OK for you to say, 'I'd like to bat like him.' But don't ever admire him. He is *not* an admirable man."

That conversation stayed with my son. Years later that same ball player got involved in a gambling scandal, and Travis remembered my words. When the front pages announced the grim tragedy, Travis said to me, "You remember what you told me about that man? You were right, Dad. You were sure right."

I was thrilled! Every father delights in those rare moments when he is actually right about something. Beyond that, I was glad for Travis and for society.

We must get right perspective to discern that which is worthy from that which is unworthy. We must see beyond popularity, past screaming crowds, more than mere wealth. Remember, he who honors the dishonorable and he who esteems the righteous too lowly are both an abomination to God.

REVERENCE, REBELLION AND WITCHCRAFT

A passage in Leviticus gives wonderful insights into levels of reverence.

> Ye shall not eat any thing with the blood: neither shall ye use enchantment, nor observe times. Ye shall not round the corners of your heads, neither shalt thou mar the corners of thy beard. Ye shall not make any cuttings in your flesh for the dead, nor print any marks upon you: I am the LORD. Do not prostitute thy daughter, to cause her to be a whore; lest the land fall to whoredom, and the land become full of wickedness. Ye shall keep my sabbaths, and reverence my sanctuary: I am the LORD. Regard not them that have familiar spirits, neither seek after wizards, to be defiled by them: I am the LORD your God. Thou shalt rise up before the hoary head [gray-haired man], and honour the face of the old man, and fear thy God: I am the LORD.
>
> —LEVITICUS 19:26–32

Notice the flow of the passage. The text has to do with assigning worth and establishing levels of reverence.

1. **Reverence life and the body:** Do not eat blood. Do not cut your hair or beard in bizarre pagan fashions. Do not cut or tattoo your flesh.

2. **Reverence relationships and sex:** Do not dishonor your family. Do not make sex pornographic. Do not sell your body or the bodies of others.

3. **Reverence the things of God:** Do not make light of those things that pertain unto God.

4. **Reverence age:** Do not do violence or show disrespect to elders. Their wisdom comes from God, and they can show you the way.

Notice in the passage from Leviticus 19, how many of the exhortations end with the words "I am the LORD." In other words, the body is important and to be respected because God made it! Respect the aged because God is their maker and judge and because they are, in His established order, closer to entering His presence than younger people are.

The postmodern contempt and even hatred for the elderly is a monstrosity of irreverence. The society that despises its elderly hates both its past *and* its future. A generation that denies respect to its elderly and protection to its unborn has denied God's ownership upon human life. Weakness and frailty become the signal to attack. Affluent mothers turn hired assassins loose on the fruit of their own wombs, and rebellious teens mock and mug grandparents in the parks.

Look back at the passage from Leviticus. What is the purpose of including the oddly placed reference to witchcraft in the midst of a teaching about respect and reverence? There is a connection between common irreverence, disrespect and witchcraft, which is rebellion against God. The New Age movement is nothing new. New Age philosophy is simply ancient witchcraft born of rebellious irreverence. The New Age movement is simply an attempt to bypass the sovereign will and omniscience of God. Refusal to submit is rebellion, and rebellion is witchcraft.

Humility and gratitude are the enabling catalysts of a true spirit of reverence. When men see themselves in right perspective with God and the things of God, they see who they are in Him and have a proper estimation of themselves. In right relation to Him, we find humility. Respect for elders, dignitaries and authority is not merely a social issue, nor is it a matter of changing manners. It is a spiritual issue. The spirit of rebellion is the malevolent cousin of witchcraft.

Respect for high office must also be taught. It is important for students to know that teachers are to be respected. The principal is to be respected, as are elders, presidents, police, mayors and aldermen. Respect for the office, even if I disagree with the man, assigns worth to office, which transcends personality.

REVERENCE AND SEX

Reverence based on the authorship of God lends meaning to life and relationships. Without a biblical view of reverence, the most shallow and superficial things in life may be afforded huge respect. Meanwhile things, people, offices and ideas of monumental importance may be trod under foot like garbage. Often the problem is in knowing whether society is making a thing too important or making it altogether unimportant.

For example, reverence for sex is a deeply confused issue. Even among those opposed to pornography and prostitution there are many who do not understand why these are evil. Pornography does not make sex more important than God. That is a common misconception about the "philosophy" of pornography. That is not what pornography is about. Pornography makes sex so low and common and animalistic that we may treat it any way we want. Pornography is based on the premise that sex is unimportant. The biblical response is not that sex is so dirty that we dare not mention it in church. The reason pornography is wrong is not because sex is wrong. The reason pornography is wrong is because it makes sex too unimportant. Pornography does not reverence sex. The Bible does. Sex is important because it was made by God. Hugh Hefner did not invent sex. God invented sex, and He was in a nifty mood that day. Sex is a good thing, a holy thing, not to be used without the reverence it deserves.

The Book of Proverbs says there are things in Creation that are absolutely wonderful, things such as a graceful ship plowing the sea, the aerodynamics of an eagle and a snake's effortless movement upon a stone. The writer marvels at such wonders of God. Last of all, he mentions sex: "the way of a man with a maid" (Prov. 30:19). That, says the writer of Proverbs, is equally wonderful, just as beautiful, important and holy as an eagle in the sky.

REVERENCE AND LIFE

We must reverence life itself. The reason abortion is wrong is because human life is the creation of God. To do away with life selfishly because we have our perspective of worth out of order is to touch the apple of God's eye. Life must be valued over convenience, over finances, over reputation and over relationships. Life is holy because God made life. When self-interest is worth more than life, character gives way to madness.

Psalm 89:7–11 is a magnificent insight:

> God is greatly to be feared in the assembly of the saints, and to be had in reverence of all them that are about him. O LORD God of hosts, who is a strong LORD like unto thee? or to thy faithfulness round about thee? Thou rulest the raging of the sea: when the waves thereof arise, thou stillest them. Thou hast broken Rahab in pieces, as one that is slain; thou hast scattered thine enemies with thy strong arm. The heavens are thine, the earth also is thine: as for the world and the fulness thereof, thou hast founded them.

In these words we see that in reverencing God, Creation, the whole natural order, the very cosmos is seen in its proper perspective. The world now makes sense because it is made by God. I now make sense because I am made by God. Birth has meaning. Death has meaning. Precious in the sight of God is the death of His saints. Everything is restored to order. For the reverent, there is discipline, creativity and divine order in the universe.

When men and nations drift into irreverence, their very

reason for living is lost. Ultimately insanity awaits when character loses reverence. When I know God is ultimately worthy, my sense of worthship is restored. When my sense of worthship is restored, my longing to worship comes again. If society assigns ultimate worth to anything except God Himself, reverence turns to madness and madness to despair. The Bible is perfectly clear. This world and the heavens that we see will burn with fire. If I reverence that which will disappear, I make myself temporary.

Many years ago my family was driving through north Mexico on a missions trip. In the middle of the night on a lonely highway a herd of cows suddenly appeared in the road. I stopped to let them get across, but another car filled with men shot around us and hit the cattle full speed. One of those cows was killed instantly. The men tumbled out of their car and stared down at the dead beast, then jumped back in their car and sped away into the night.

From the back seat our little boy said, "Dad, remember when we were in India how the people reverenced the cattle?"

"Yes," I said. "I remember that."

He said, "I don't want any god that can be killed by a Chevy."

If I am fixed on that which is unshakable, and the strength of my character rests thereon, then "when all around my soul gives way, He then is all my Hope and Stay."[2]

The Cossacks, more bored than angry, sat on their horses and stared up at the slate sky, muttering to themselves that snow—probably lots of snow—was on its way. They were warriors, made for pitched battles and desperate cavalry charges, not policemen fit for herding Jews for cattle. The czar wanted this Semitic rabble moved, and they would move them, but it was boring, cold, unsoldierly work; they would not pretend to like it.

"You, there," Sergeant Ivanovich barked, his breath a white-hot cloud. "Hurry it up. That will not break, you know. Just throw it on the cart, and get on with it."

"No," the old rabbi answered, "it will not break. It can be broken, but it will not break."

Sergeant Ivanovich snorted and shrugged. Why did the czar hate these Jews? Ivanovich could not understand it. Then again, he could not understand the Jews either. It can be broken, but it will not break. What nonsense.

"I don't have time for riddles, you old fool. Just toss it up there."

Ignoring him, the rabbi continued, without hurrying, to wrap carefully the long-handled rolls as if they were made of crystal. If the old man was frightened of Ivanovich, it was not apparent. What was apparent was that whatever was in the odd, tube-like rolls was precious to the ancient rabbi.

"What have you got there anyway?" Ivanovich demanded.

"The Torah."

"What?"

"The Torah," the old man repeated, looking for the first time at the young Cossack sergeant. "Do you know what that means... Torah?"

"Is it valuable?"

"No, not as you mean valuable. You could not get even a few rubles for this ragged old scroll. It determines the value of all else, but it is of little value itself. There, I'm finished."

"Good, toss it up there and get your people moving."

"I will carry it," the rabbi said.

"For three hundred miles?"

"It has carried me for seventy-eight years and my people before me for thousands of years. I can carry it for a few hundred miles."

Ivanovich shrugged. "Suit yourself."

"Never," the rabbi muttered, but Ivanovich pretended not to hear. Instead he spun his horse and charged back down the ragged column of carts filled with the pathetic little the Jews owned. The burly sergeant knew in his heart that the czar was miscalculating. There was no use persecuting people like this, people who, owning nothing of value, would carry a tattered scroll as if it were pure gold.

CHAPTER 10

GRATITUDE:
CHARACTER IN CELEBRATION

Her evangelistic ministry was just beginning to find a wide public platform when Kathryn Kuhlman was blindsided by what might have derailed her. Though separated for years from her first husband, she was not seeking a divorce. When he sued for divorce in Arizona, she was in an extended and powerfully anointed crusade in Franklin, Ohio. If word of the divorce had hit the front page, she would have been finished. In 1948, a divorced, single female evangelist was not possible.

The papers were served on her by the county sheriff personally. She was devastated. Her past had erupted into her present with the power to destroy her future. With a trembling hand she received the papers from the sheriff, but when she looked into his eyes, Kuhlman was shocked to find tender mercy.

"My office ordinarily releases the names of all divorce suits to the local newspaper," he explained. "But I have been attending your services and am convinced God sent you to this crime-riddled county for a special purpose. There is no need for anyone but the two of us to know what has happened. God bless you and your ministry among us. I am at your service."

The young female preacher was overcome with gratitude. She told the burly peace officer, "I will be grateful to you for the rest of my life."

Seven years later when the "news" of her divorce finally broke in the Akron newspaper, it was old news, and her ministry was far too strong for the story to do much damage. The sheriff had given her the time she needed, and she never forgot him.

Every year, until the day of his death nearly a quarter of a century later, that burly sheriff received an expensive flower arrangement on his birthday. The card always said the same thing: "With gratitude from Kathryn Kuhlman."[1]

Gratitude is merely the secret hope of further favors.

—FRANCOIS DE LA ROCHEFOUCAULD

THE BOOKS IN THE HOMER Smith series are among the better ones ever written. Homer Smith, the protagonist, was an itinerant black carpenter from the Southern part of the United States. The most famous of these books is *The Lilies of the Field*, immortalized in cinema by Sidney Poitier, who, for his role in that film, won an Academy Award for best actor in 1963.

Homer Smith was not a particularly educated man, but he was a Christian man with a great deal of wisdom. In *The Lilies of the Field* the other main character was a German Mother Superior shepherding a small band of four or five nuns in the desert of New Mexico. Hoping to build a church there in the desert, this curmudgeonly old nun was working her fingers to the bone and praying that God would send her a means to get her chapel built. When Homer Smith drove up in his battered station wagon, she was convinced he was the instrument of God. The crotchety old German nun badgered, cajoled, coaxed and tricked Homer Smith into building her church.

Despite all that, however, she refused to tell Smith "thank you." Near the end of the book, by the use of an English lesson, Homer Smith tricked that old nun into saying "thank you." For the first time in her life—to man, woman or child—she said, "Thank you," and she found it a jolting experience![2]

Gratitude is not only among the very highest virtues; it is

synonymous with the deepest, most profound elements of scriptural holiness. Gratitude is of that spiritual universe that includes humility, contentment and praise. Gratitude is diametrically opposed to pride.

Some years ago I was counseling with a teenager who had been raised from infancy by his grandparents. The boy's father had been killed in an automobile accident, and subsequently his mother disappeared. The grandparents had been doing all they could for him at great expense to themselves. It is difficult for anyone to raise a teenager, and people in their sixties and seventies ought not to have to go through it a second time around.

For several years he rewarded them with unfathomable rebellion, anger and sin until he made his grandparents miserable. I told him, "They did not have to take you in. You could have gone to an orphanage. You could have been a ward of the court. They got up with you in the middle of the night. They changed your diapers and fed you and clothed you. They raised you at great sacrifice to themselves. Nobody would have blamed them if they had said, 'We just can't handle it at our age.'"

He replied bitterly, "Do you think this is the first time I've ever thought of all that? I know what they've done. What am I supposed to do, spend the rest of my life saying 'thank you'?"

Well, yes! Yes! A thousand times *yes*! You're supposed to spend the rest of your life saying "thank you." Everyone is. That is what real life is, an expression of gratitude to God. *Yes*, we are supposed to spend the rest of our lives, every waking moment, saying "thank you." That is what the apostle Paul said. "I consider myself to be in debt, both to the Greek and to the non-Greek. I am indebted to the whole world. I am in debt to *God*!" (See Romans 1:14.)

When I consider my own life, I must ask, "Who am I to preach the unsearchable riches of Christ?" These are the same feet that hurried to do sin. These hands were covered with blood. Single-handedly I very nearly destroyed my family and myself. Yet God scooped me up out of the gutter of the universe, hosed me down and filled me with the Holy Spirit. He gave me back my soul and my sanity. He gave me another chance with my family and allowed me the privilege to preach the Word of His kingdom. Amazing! Yes. Yes, the rest of my life *is* a "thank you."

The reason we resist the life of unending gratitude is fear that "thank you" implies responsibility. What the corrupt character wants is to be free from the responsibility to, in any way, "pay some of it back." The great tragedy of the affluent West is its pathetic ingrates, the affluent who think that somehow or other they deserve it all.

A Sin of the Rich

Ingratitude is, in general, not a sin of the poor, but of the rich, and we are rich. Look at us. A kid who has never had anything and has no hope of having anything, who wakes up cold every morning of his life in a tar paper shack, is likely to be grateful for the apple he gets at Christmas. The kid who wakes up every morning in a $350,000 house and who has never worked a day in his life, who puts hundreds of dollars' worth of clothes on his well-scrubbed back every morning and is driven to a private school (that somebody else is paying for), complains about the laptop he gets for Christmas because it does not have all the bells and whistles he wanted.

I remember one Christmas season in Ghana, West Africa. At the home of a college president, a sophisticated, educated Ghanaian trapped in a nation on the brink of a nightmare, I learned much about gratitude.

In 1980 there was nothing in Ghana. The borders were closed. The shelves of the stores were empty, and the people were hungry. Christmas Eve was also the birthday of the eldest son, a senior at his father's college. No one had a single present to give him.

I myself had little with me. I was actually living as they were living, but I wanted to give that boy something for his birthday. I took a used T-shirt out of my luggage, washed it, folded it, put it in a box with an American ten-dollar bill and wrapped it with plain brown paper.

At supper, I handed the boy his one modest gift, and if I live to be one hundred, I will never forget that college student weeping with gratitude over a used T-shirt and a ten-dollar bill.

THE DAUGHTERS OF THE HORSELEACH

> The horseleach hath two daughters, crying, Give, give. There are three things that are never satisfied, yea, four things say not, It is enough: The grave; and the barren womb; the earth that is not filled with water; and the fire that saith not, It is enough.
>
> —PROVERBS 30:15–16

The daughters of the horseleach are never satisfied, and they never say "thank you." They continue to demand more and more blood. Never satiated, never grateful, never content, their possessive lust is a bottomless pit.

Ingratitude, a curse to everyone it touches, is a corrupting habit that destroys character. The child taken for ice cream complains because there are no chocolate sprinkles on top. Nothing is ever quite right. Nothing is ever quite enough. Parents save and sacrifice to take their children to Disney World, and the children think that somehow that is their just due in life. It seldom dawns on them that, out of their love for them, their parents are spending, perhaps, the worst week of their entire lives. Even less frequently does it occur to American children this is something for which they actually ought to be grateful.

Parents pay an exorbitant entry fee to a theme park, fork

over five dollars for a hot dog that tastes like sawdust and go on rides that make them wish they were dead. At the end of the day the parents, exhausted and dead broke, want only to know that their children are happy and grateful. The well-developed character says, "This is more than I deserve. This is perfect." Not, "This will do." Not, "OK, I guess." But, "Thanks! This is perfect, and I do *not* deserve perfect."

Ingratitude is actually a form of selfishness, and it can be devastating to the feelings of others.

A funeral I preached a few years ago was one of the truly discouraging moments of my ministry. A lovely Christian woman, an elderly lady, had died suddenly and left behind a husband who was not strong in the Lord and who had only attended the church a few times.

Her casket was literally blanketed in the most beautiful roses I have ever seen in my life. I commented to the husband, "Sir, I have never seen roses like these. These are beautiful."

He said, "You know, preacher, Margaret loved roses. She was a real sentimental sort of woman. She always wanted me to buy her roses. 'Buy me some roses, buy me roses,' she always used to say.

"I'm not really into that sort of thing," he explained. "I never did buy her roses. I guess I just didn't want to waste money and time on stuff like that.

"Well," he said brightly, his moist eyes shining, "I'm making it up to her now."

The fool! He was not making it up to her. He was pouring salve on his own conscience.

Husband, buy her the roses *now*. Don't lean over a coffin and say the words you always meant to say. "Oh, honey, I think you're wonderful!" Tell her now!

Children, do not face the day that your mother says, "Daddy isn't coming home from work. Something terrible happened at the office," only to realize that you never said, "Thanks, Dad."

Don't get to be forty before you suddenly realize that the clothes you've always worn did not get magically washed. I do not know who I thought was washing my clothes when I was a teenager. The only thing I knew was that they appeared in my chest of drawers every week. *Now* I realize that the brownies were not in there doing the laundry. I did not deserve a mother who washed my clothes until I graduated from high school. I do not deserve the wife who does it now.

There are American teens who would rather stay home from school than show up in discount-store tennis shoes. Life's critical issue in the West has become the brand name on our tennis shoes. In Rwanda today, there are teens who pray, "O God, just once before I die, could I wear a pair of shoes? Any kind of shoes?"

This is not to heap on guilt. It is rather to say that we must awaken to the reality that we are in debt. We are the richest, most powerful, most prosperous, most educated, cleanest, healthiest people who have ever been on the face of the earth. At times we can also be the most selfish, self-centered, ungrateful people who have ever lived.

HABITUAL GRATITUDE

All ingratitude is basically ingratitude to God. God blesses us with health, happiness and the joy of children, but we sulk because we are not the president of the United States. We pray for a job, and when we get one, we whine about the pay. There are people, millions of people, who would give anything in the world just for a job, any job. A woman prays for a new house and resents having to clean it. A single woman prays without ceasing to get married and then lives in sullen depression because her long-awaited husband is not perfect.

We are seldom just plain, bottom-line grateful to God. God gives us the strawberry sundae, and we complain because it does not have whipped cream. He gives us the whipped cream, and we moan for a cherry on top. At some point we must dare to defeat the spirit of the horseleach and say, "It is *enough*. I am content with this. It is more than I deserve."

Gratitude as well as ingratitude can become a habit of life. We can begin to see everything that happens to us as an opportunity to praise God. Gratitude can be added to character.

Leonard Ravenhill told of a minister visiting a horrible insane asylum in the United Kingdom sometime in the latter part of the nineteenth century. As the minister walked in the front door, a man in a second-story window pressed his head through the bars and shouted down to the visitor below, "Have you thanked God today?"

"I have," the pastor answered.

"Aye," the inmate said, "but have you thanked Him for your sanity?"

We must get specific with God. Instead of complaining about the rain, thank God that you are alive. Instead of complaining about your husband, thank God you are not lonely. Instead of complaining about having to wear this or that kind of shirt, thank God you have a shirt. Gratitude is a learned way of life. It is the open hand instead of the clenched fist. It is saying, *Yours*, and not, *Mine*. It is the Spirit of Jesus and not the spirit of the world.

Character is not built by just grimly obeying the rules. It is learned best by celebrating the joy of God's grace. Character lived or taught in a rules-oriented method destroys joy. The celebration of character development is not a burdensome duty, nor is it the lash of the cruel taskmaster. There is joy and meaning to be found in serving God, who has given us more than we could ever pay back. The character to live in celebrational gratitude is the key to happy significance.

A mighty raja in ancient India had a gardener who was a chronic thief. The nobleman overlooked it for years because the gardener never stole anything very precious. Finally, however, the man stole one of the crown jewels. After prying a ruby of inestimable value out of the royal crown, the wicked gardener fled in the night on a horse stolen from the stable. In the dark, as he rode the nobleman's horse wildly out of the royal compound, he trampled the nobleman's son and killed him.

Some days later the raja's soldiers captured the deadly thief and dragged him before the raja. The executioner's broad sword poised over his neck, the penitent thief cried, "Please, mighty master, have mercy on me. Don't kill me. If not for my sake, then for my wife and five children. I plead, don't kill me."

The great and gracious raja forgave him. He forgave him not only the thievery but also the death of his son. At last he even reinstated him as gardener. Yet three months later the gardener was again hurled before the raja. He had stolen a nearly worthless cup from the royal kitchen.

The great raja said, "Bring the swordsman and cut his head off. Execute him here in my presence."

The gardener did not dare to plead for his life. Instead he said, "I deserve to die... But I don't understand. You forgive me for the death of your son. Will you now execute me for the theft of a miserable kitchen utensil?"

The raja said, "No, you really don't understand.

I'm not executing you for the theft of a cup. I'm executing you for the sin of ingratitude."

Character—true character, the life of virtue and strength—is a joyful, triumphant celebration of God's grace. Gratitude and contentment are the answers of true character to the discontented, unhappy spirit of this age. The voice of the world is the voice of the horseleach crying, "More, more, more." Character, godly character, looks up at the bleeding, dying form of Christ on the cross and humbly acknowledges, "It is more than I deserve. He *is* enough for me."

NOTES

CHAPTER 1
CHARACTER: THE ENGRAVER'S ART

1. Karl Menninger, *Whatever Became of Sin?* (New York: Hawthorn Books Inc., 1973).

CHAPTER 2
COURAGE: CHARACTER IN CRISIS

1. "U.S. soldiers rescue wounded woman on bridge," retrieved from the Internet on June 19, 2003 at www.fananews.com/kuwait/2003/Apr/01/17471002.htm.
2. Mark Armstrong, "Maher Causes 'Cowardly' Flap," *E! Online News*, retrieved from the Internet on June 19, 2003 at http://earthlink.eonline.com/News/Items/0,1,8852,00.html.
3. Bruce Olson, *Bruchko* (Lake Mary, FL: Charisma House, 1999).

CHAPTER 3
LOYALTY: CHARACTER IN COMMUNITY

1. "Chronology of Sam Houston's Life," The Sam Houston Memorial Museum, Sam Houston State University. Retrieved from the Internet on July 3, 2003 at www.shsu.edu/~smm_www/History.

CHAPTER 4
DILIGENCE: CHARACTER IN ACTION

1. "George Washington Carver," *The African American Almanac*, 7th ed. (Gale, 1997). Retrieved from the Internet on June 20, 2003 at www.galegroup.com/free_resources/bhm/bio/carver_g.htm.
2. A.W. Tozer, *The Pursuit of God* (Harrisburg, PA.: Christian Publications, 1948).

CHAPTER 5
MODESTY: CHARACTER AS SIMPLICITY

1. Author's personal observations and personal research on
    James Blanchard.

CHAPTER 6
FRUGALITY: CHARACTER AND PROSPERITY

1. "Biography of Oseola McCarty," The Mississippi Writers
    and Musicians Project at Starkville High School. Retrieved
    from the Internet on June 21, 2003 at
    www.shs.starkville.k12.ms.us/mswm/MSWriters
    AndMusicians/writers/OMcCarty.html. "McCarty Featured
    in National Magazine," *USM News*, released October 9,
    2001. Retrieved from the Internet on June 21, 2003 at
    www.pr.usm.edu/prnews/oct01/
    OMWORTH.HTM.
2. Richard Foster, *Money, Sex and Power* (San Francisco:
    Harper and Row, 1985).
3. John Wesley, "The Use of Money," in *The Collected Works of
    John Wesley* (Chicago: Baker House, n.d.).
4. Foster, *Money, Sex and Power*.

CHAPTER 7
HONESTY: CHARACTER AND TRUTH

1. "Wings of Valor—the Court Martial of Billy Mitchell."
    Retrieved from the Internet on June 21, 2003 at www.home-
    ofheroes.com/wings/part1/6_survival.html.

CHAPTER 8
MEEKNESS: CHARACTER AND POWER

1. "Second Inaugural Address of Abraham Lincoln, Saturday,
    March 4, 1865," The Avalon Project at Yale Law School.
    Retrieved from the Internet on June 22, 2003 at
    www.yale.edu/lawweb/avalon/presiden/inaug/
    lincoln2.htm.
2. Alan Jay Lerner and Frederick Loewe, *Camelot* (New York:
    Random House, 1961).

CHAPTER 9
REVERENCE: CHARACTER AND THE SACRED

1. "Closed Sundays. It's part of Chick-fil-A recipe," "We're here to serve. And no sandwiches" and "Fact Sheet," Chick-fil-A website. Retrieved from the Internet on June 24, 2003 at www.chick-fil-a.com.
2. "My Hope Is Built" by Edward Mote. Public domain.

CHAPTER 10
GRATITUDE: CHARACTER IN CELEBRATION

1. Jamie Buckingham, *Daughter of Destiny: Kathryn Kuhlman...Her Story* (Plainfield, NJ: Logos International, 1976), 112–113.
2. William Edmund Barrett, *The Lilies of the Field* (New York: Doubleday, 1962).